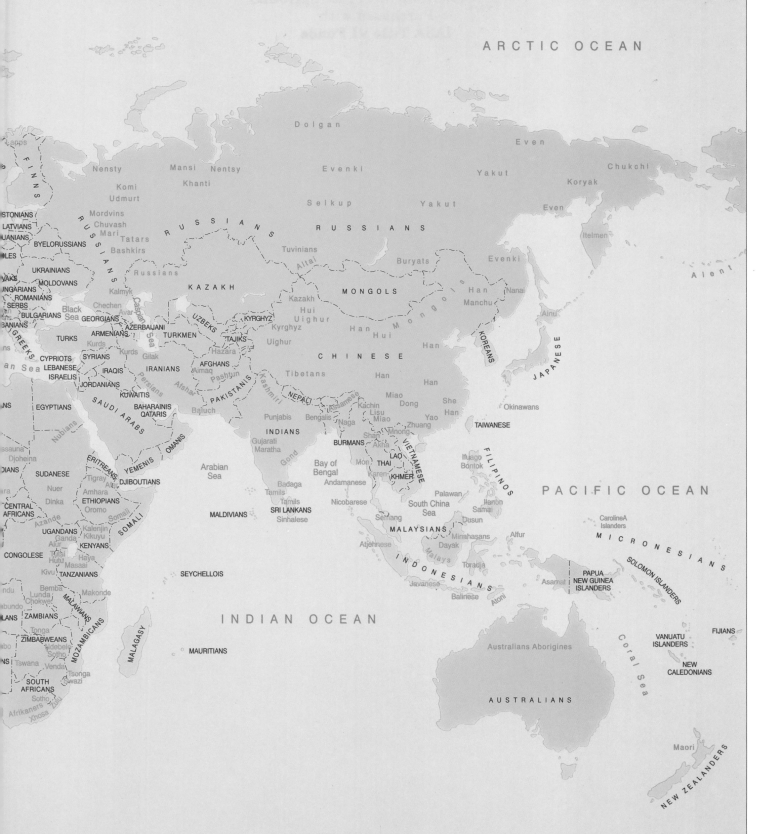

ARCTIC OCEAN

Dolgan

Even

Nensty   Mansi   Nentsy   Evenki   Yakut   Chukchi
Komi   Koryak
Khanti
Udmurt   Selkup   Yakut   Even

FINNS
Mordvins   Itelmen
ESTONIANS   Chuvash   RUSSIANS   RUSSIANS
LATVIANS   Mari
LITHUANIANS Tatars
BYELORUSSIANS Bashkirs   Tuvinians
                    Russians   Buryats   Evenki
POLES   Altai   Nanai
UKRAINIANS   KAZAKH   MONGOLS   Han
YAKS   MOLDOVANS   Kazakh   Manchu
HUNGARIANS Kalmyk   Hui   Ainu
ROMANIANS   Chechen   UZBEKS   Uighur   Han
SERBS   Avar   KYRGHYZ   Kyrghyz   Han   KOREANS
BULGARIANS Black GEORGIANS   TAJIKS   Hui
ALBANIANS   Sea   AZERBAIJANI TURKMEN   Han
GREEKS   ARMENIANS   Uighur   CHINESE   JAPANESE
TURKS   Kurds   Kurds Gilak   Tibetans   Han
CYPRIOTS SYRIANS   IRANIANS AFGHANS   Han
LEBANESE   Aimaq   Pashtun
an Sea ISRAELIS IRAQIS   Kashmiri   Miao
JORDANIANS   KUWAITIS   PAKISTANIS NEPALI   Dong   She   Okinawans
EGYPTIANS   Baluch   Punjabis Bengalis Miao Yao Han
SAUDI ARABS BAHARAINIS   Naga Zhuang   TAIWANESE
Nubians   QATARI   INDIANS   Gujarati   Shan Mnong
                              Maratha   BURMANS   Akha VIETNAMESE
ssauna ERITREANS YEMENIS OMANIS   Gond   Mon LAO FILIPINOS
Djoheina Tigray DJIBOUTIANS Arabian   Bay of   THAI KHMER
DIANS   Amhara   Sea   Badaga Bengal Karen
SUDANESE Nuer ETHIOPIANS   Tamils Andamanese South China
Dinka   Oromo   Sea
CENTRAL Azande Somali   MALDIVIANS Tamils Nicobarese
AFRICANS   SRI LANKANS
UGANDANS Kalenjin KENYANS SOMALI   Sinhalese   Semang
CONGOLESE Ganda Kikuyu   MALAYSIANS
Aluf   Tutsi Haya   SEYCHELLOIS   INDONESIANS
Kivu   Hutu Masaai   Javanese
Bemba TANZANIANS
Makonde
Lunda
Chokwe MALAWIANS   INDIAN OCEAN
ZAMBIANS   MAURITIANS
Tonga
ZIMBABWEANS Ndebele
Sotho   MALAGASY
Tswana Venda
SOUTH   Tsonga
AFRICANS Swazi
Sotho   Zulu
Afrikaners
Xhosa

PACIFIC OCEAN

CarolineA
Islanders
MICRONESIANS
SOLOMON ISLANDERS

PAPUA
NEW GUINEA
ISLANDERS

Coral
Sea

VANUATU
ISLANDERS   FIJIANS

NEW
CALEDONIANS

Australians Aborigines

AUSTRALIANS

Maori

NEW ZEALANDERS

PEOPLES of the WORLD
customs and cultures

Editor
Amiram Gonen

Educational Editor
Barbara P. Sutnick

Volume 3
Cehi-Endo

Grolier Educational
SHERMAN TURNPIKE, DANBURY, CONNECTICUT

Managing Editor
Rachel Gilon

Library of Congress Cataloging-in-Publication Data

Peoples of the world : customs and cultures.

p.   cm.

Includes bibliographical references and index.

Summary: An encyclopedia of world peoples, combining historical and current, anthropological and social, and other information on the status of ethnic groups worldwide.

ISBN 0-7172-9236-3 (set)

1. Ethnology—Encyclopedia, Juvenile   [1. Ethnology-Encyclopedias.]   1. Grolier Educational Corporation.

GN333,P46 1998

306' .03—dc21

97-32980

CIP

AC

Published 1998 by Grolier Educational
Sherman Turnpike, Danbury, Connecticut

© 1998 G.G. The Jerusalem Publishing House Ltd.
39 Tchernechovski St.
P.O.B. 7147,
Jerusalem, 91071
Israel

Set ISBN 0-7172-9236-3
Volume 3: ISBN 0-7172-9239-8

For information, address the publisher:
Grolier Educational. Sherman Turnpike, Danbury, Connecticut 06816

Cover design by Smart Graphics
Planned and produced by The Jerusalem Publishing House, Jerusalem
Printed in China

CEHI see CZECHS.

CELE A group among the NGUNI of southern Africa.

CENTRAL AFRICANS The Central African Republic is a country in Africa that received independence in 1960. There are 2.8 million people there, mostly in the western half of the country; hardly any people live in large parts of the eastern half. There are about 80 **ethnic** groups in the country. Most of these groups came to the area in several waves during the eighteenth and nineteenth centuries. The largest ethnic group is the BANDA, who live in the center and eastern regions. Other groups include: the BAYA, who live in the northern and western areas; the AZANDE, in the southeast; the SARA, which is also the strongest **ethnic** group in Chad, who live in the north; the MANDJIA in the center; the MBUM, in the northwest; the MBAKA, in the southwest; the YAKOMBA, SANGO, and GBANZIRI, who all live along the Ubangi River; and the PYGMIES, who live in the farthest part of the southwest.

Religion and language: About 60 percent of the population practice traditional religions. Thirty-five percent are Christians, and five percent are Muslims.

The official languages of the Central African Republic are French and Sango. Sango was used as a language common to all in the area during the time when Europeans came to Africa. Since then it has become the national language of the country.

Peoples and politics: The Yakomba, Sango, and Gbanziri are very important ethnic groups. They play an important role in the economy, government, and society of the country. Even though they make up only about five percent of the population, they held 60 percent of the government jobs when the FRENCH were in control of the area. They continued to be important after the Central Africans won their freedom from the FRENCH.

When the Central African Republic gained independence in 1960, a political party mostly made up of members of the Baya group took control of the government. They did not allow any other political parties to be part of the government or to exist. In 1965 Jean-Bedel Bokassa, who was a member of the Mbaka group, overthrew the government and took control. At first, the Baya group supported Bokassa because he had made a Baya the head of the army. However, they took away their support when Bokassa had the Baya army leader killed. Bokassa ruled with total control. He was overthrown in 1979 by a revolt in which no one was killed. The first president then regained power. The country still has only one political party. However, the people of the country have called for changes in the governing process.

CEWA see CHEWA.

CHABA A group among the EGBA in southwestern Nigeria.

CHACHI see CAYAPAS.

CHADIANS The Chadians are the people who live in the African country of Chad. There are 5.5 million of them, many of whom live in the southern half of the country. About half of them are Muslims, seven percent are Christians, and the rest follow traditional religions. French is the official language of Chad. However, the most widely spoken languages are Arabic and Sara.

Chad is one of the poorest and least modern countries in Africa. It gained freedom from the FRENCH in 1960. Since then there has been much arguing and misunderstanding between the Chadians who live in the northern part of the country and those who live in the south. The people of the north are mostly Muslims. They are **nomads** or sometimes nomads, and come from an ARAB background. They speak Arabic particularly for business and also other languages of the area. The two main **ethnic** groups that live in the north are the HASSAUNA, in the northwest, and the DJOHEINA, in the northeast. These two groups are divided into many smaller family groups. They fight a lot among themselves. These groups speak a Chadian version of Arabic.

The southern part of Chad is smaller but has more people living there. There is also a better water supply in the south. Most of the people in the south are members of the SARA people. The Sara are farmers who live in permanent settlements. The Sara group is divided into several smaller groups with similar cultures and languages. The other people in the south belong to many smaller ethnic groups. They include: the MOUNDANG, TOUBOURI, MASA, MUSGUM, MASALIT, MABA, and the LISI. The Maba and Lisi groups are divided even further into smaller parts.

Since the end of World War II the people of the south have become more modern and educated. Many people learned to read, and many became Christian. The people of the north did not want modern education and stayed with the Muslim religion. Because of this difference most of the government workers came from the south after Chad became independent. The northern people did not mind being ruled by the French, but they did not want the southerners to take control. This argument between the north and south made the government in Chad weak. Since gaining its independence, Chad has had three civil wars. Each time the French stepped in to stop the fighting.

CHAGA (also called Chagga) The Chaga are a people who live in the southeastern part of Tanzania. There are about one million of them. They are the third-largest **ethnic** group in Tanzania. The Chaga language is part of the Bantu group, which is part of the Niger-Congo family. The Chaga area is called Chagaland or Uchaga. The main part of Chagaland is on the southern hillsides of Mount Kilimanjaro.

Economy and culture: The Chaga are one of the most modern and educated ethnic groups in Tanzania. They are strongly involved in modern education, the coffee business, and in working for others, as well as in Tanzanian politics. Some Chaga are Roman Catholics, and others are Lutheran Protestants.

Before Europeans came to Africa, the Chaga were divided into 30 separate groups. Each group was led by a chief. Some of these groups fought over who would control the right to trade with people on the coast.

Chagaland has a very good climate and environment, and soil that is watered well. This allows the Chaga to do a lot of farming. They use natural materials for fertilizer. They grow bananas for food and also produce coffee and other crops to sell.

Men are the leaders in Chaga families, and one man will often have more than one wife. Both men and women work equally in the Chaga society. Different responsibilities and privileges are given to people based on their age group. The Chaga hate slavery.

CHAGGA see CHAGA.

CHAHA A group among the GURAGE in central Ethiopia.

CHAHAR AIMAQ see AIMAQ.

CHAHAR (CHAR) LANG A large **clan** of the BAKHTIARI in southwestern Iran.

CHAKHESANG The Chakhesang are an **ethnic** group that lives in the Phek region of Nagaland, India. They speak Chokri, which is part of the Naga language group of the Tibeto-Burman language family.

The Chakhesang are part of the Indo-Mongoloid group. However, they are considered by the BRITISH to be Eastern ANGAMI, because they follow most Angami customs and marry Angami people. The name Chakhesang is a combination of the first parts of the names of three small tribes. These are: the CHAKHUMA and KHEZAMA (who are both Southern Angami) and SANGTAM. The name was created in 1948 when the three tribes joined together to become one group.

The Chakhesang farm by cutting terraces into mountainsides for planting. They produce two crops a year.

CHAKHUMA A group among the CHAKHESANG in Nagaland, eastern India.

CHAKMA The Chakma are a people of about 600,000 who live in India, in the northeast hilly areas of the states of Assam, Meghalaya, Mizoram, Tripura, and West Bengal, as well as in Bangladesh. They are about equally divided in number between India and Bangladesh. In 1981 there were 75,000 Chakma. They speak Bengali, which is a member of the Indo-Aryan language family.

Religion: The Chakma are Buddhists. They also practice their traditional customs, especially for births, marriages, and burials by burning. They have their own alphabet and also their own religious book called the *Taras.*

Culture: The Chakma, and other people who live in the hills, come from different **ethnic** groups than those who live in permanent settlements. They are a MONGOLOID people. Their culture is similar to the culture of the hill people living in the area from Tibet to Thailand.

The Chakma build their houses completely out of bamboo. The houses are set on a high platform, also made of bamboo, which stands about 12 feet off the ground.

The Chakma are mostly farmers who use a special form of planting on the hillside. They grow rice, melon, cucumber, chili, eggplant, corn, sesame, and cotton seeds, all mixed together in the same fields. Each crop comes out in its own season and is harvested without any more planting. In the nineteenth century the Chakma who lived by the river began to use the plow. However, those that live further inland still prepare their land for farming by cutting down and burning any natural growth (slash-and-burn agriculture). The Chakma are also good weavers.

CHAM The Cham are a people of about 300,000 who live mostly in the southern part of Vietnam and Cambodia. There are 220,000 Cham in Cambodia and 60,000 in Vietnam. The rest are found in nearby Malaysia and Thailand. They speak the Cham language, which is a member of the Malayo-Polynesian family. Even though today there are not many Cham, in the past their Champa state had a strong influence on the customs and traditions of people living nearby.

Language: The Cham group was one of the first in the area to create its own alphabet, which was based on Indian writing. It is still used today, even though the FRENCH, who used to rule the region, introduced the Roman alphabet (used for English), which is becoming popular.

Cham

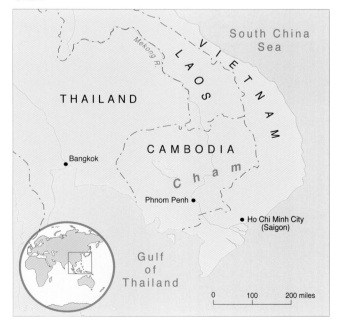

Religion and culture: When the Champa Empire was at its most powerful, two cultures influenced it the most: the Hindus of India and the Muslims. Today the Cham living in Vietnam practice their own versions of both the Hindu and Muslim religions. The two religions affect one another's customs and beliefs. The Cham living in Cambodia practice a stricter form of Islam.

History: The Cham state in the southern part of Vietnam, Champa, was very successful until the fifteenth century. The Cham were separated between Vietnam and Cambodia in 1471, when the VIETNAMESE invaded Champa. The richer Cham fled to Cambodia, while the poor farmers stayed in Vietnam.

In the past few years the Cham have again begun to take pride in their **ethnic** group. This changed because the government has promised them some self-rule. In the 1960s a secret group was created called the Front for the Liberation of Champa. They were dedicated to bringing about Champan independence.

Culture: The Cham still farm and sell their crops. However, bad weather and poor land make it hard to grow rice. For hundreds of years the Cham have adopted the cultures of the surrounding peoples and stopped speaking their own language, except in hard-to-reach villages. (see also HROY)

CHAMALAL The Chamalal are an **ethnic** group that lives in the northwestern part of Daghestan in the Russian Federation. They make their homes in the valley where the Andian Koisu branch of the Sulak River flows. There are 5,000 Chamalal.

The language of the Chamalal is part of the Avar-Andi-Dido branch of the north Caucasian family. It does not have an alphabet or a written form; Avarian is used as the written language. The Chamalal have practiced the Sunni branch of the Muslim religion that is part of the Shafi'i school since the sixteenth century.

The Chamalal have been considered a group among the AVAR people since the 1930s. Today they are part of a movement trying to bring together the related groups that live in the Avarian region. They call themselves both "Chamalal" and "Avar."

The Chamalal economy includes farming, gardening, cattle-breeding, and home businesses.

CHAMARRO see MARIANA ISLANDERS.

CHAMBA A group among the TIV in northern Nigeria.

CHAMBRI The Chambri are an **ethnic** group that lives in the northern part of Papua New Guinea, on an island mountain in the Sepik River valley. There are a few thousand Chambri. They speak a local Sepik language. They live on fish that they catch in the waters off their island. Most of the Chambri are Catholic. However, they still believe that all power comes from the spirits of the dead. They are mostly fishing people but also raise chickens and catch turtles.

CHAMORROS The Chamorros are an **ethnic** group that lives in Guam and in the nearby Mariana Islands in the Pacific Ocean. There are about 100,000 Chamorros: 80,000 in Guam and 20,000 in the Mariana Islands. They speak Chamorro among themselves. Chamorro is an Austronesian language that is mixed with Spanish, Tagalog (Filipino), and English. However, they speak English with outsiders. The Chamorros are mainly Roman Catholics.

CHAMPA see KHAMPA.

CHAMULA The Chamula are a group of about 50,000 that is native to the mountainous region of Chiapas, Mexico. They speak the Tzotzil language, which is part of the Mayan family. Most live in the village of San Juan Chamula,

A Chamulan man

A Chamulan woman

which is northwest of the town of San Cristobal de las Casas.

Religion: Outwardly the Chamula are Roman Catholics. However, their beliefs and practices still have many aspects of their traditional religion. For example, they believe that Jesus rose from the cross and became the sun. Their carnival before the season of Lent is not only Christian but also marks five "lost days" from the ancient calendar of the Mayan people.

The Chamula fought very hard against the SPANIARDS who invaded their area in 1524. However, the Spanish succeeded in conquering the Chamula by 1528. The Chamula were forced to work for Spanish landowners. They rebelled in 1869 because they were upset about losing the war of independence, were very poor, and did not feel part of the new country of Mexico. Until recently, the Chamula who lived in towns were treated as a lower group by the *mestizos,* who are the children of one white and one Indian parent. However, lately it seems that people are beginning to accept Indians more. The Chamulan farmers are getting poorer as time goes on, so they often have to leave their homeland to look for other work. (see also MAYA)

CHAN (call themselves Lazi) The Chan are an **ethnic** group of about 30,000 that mainly lives in seven villages in Turkey. They are found between the Chozokh River valley and the coast of the Black Sea. There are also Chan who live in the Ajarian Region of Georgia. They were Eastern Orthodox Christians from the sixth until the sixteenth century. After that time they began to follow the Sunni branch of the Muslim religion that is part of the Hanafi school.

The languages spoken by the Chan and the MEGREL group are now considered two **dialects** of Megrel-Chan, which is also called Zan and is part of the Caucasian family. The Chan living in Georgia use Georgian as their written language; those living in Turkey use Turkish. They mainly farm, fish, and trade.

In scientific studies the name Laz is sometimes used instead of Chan. Both the Chan and Megrel groups are also called Zan.

CHANA A Native South American group in Argentina.

CHANG A NAGA group of over 15,000 people who live in the hills of Nagaland, on the border between the eastern part of India and the northwestern part of Myanmar (formerly called Burma).

CHARA The Chara are an **ethnic** group of about 15,000 that lives in the eastern part of Kefar Province, Ethiopia, between the Dintsha and Omo rivers. Their language is part of the Omotic group. The Chara practice traditional religious beliefs. They farm grain and the bananalike ensete plant.

CHARCA A group among the AYMARA in western South America.

CHAVANTE see XAVANTE.

CHAVCHU A group among the CHUKCHI in northeast Siberia.

CHAVCHYVAV A group among the KORYAK in northeast Siberia. Traditionally, the Chavchyvav were fisherman.

CHAZICHE A tiny group among the TEHUELCHE. Almost all the Chaziche have died out.

CHECHEN (call themselves Nokhchiy) The Chechen are a people who live in the western part of Daghestan. They are found in the central Caucasus Mountains, mainly between the middle course of the Terek River and the main Caucasian

Chechen

Ridge. In 1989 there were 960,000 Chechen. Of these 734,000 lived in the Chechen-Ingush Autonomous Republic, which was divided between Chechnya and Ingushetia in the early 1990s. There are also Chechen communities found in Turkey (about 7,000) and in Jordan (about 4,000).

Religion: During the seventh and eighth centuries the Chechen adopted Eastern Orthodox Christianity under the influence of Georgia. Since the sixteenth and seventeenth centuries they have been Sunni Muslims of the Hanafi school.

Language: The Chechen language belongs to the Vakh (or Veinakh) branch of the north Caucasian family. It is the largest North Caucasian language. In 1925 their writing used a form of the Roman alphabet (used for English). Since 1938 they have used the Cyrillic alphabet (used for Russian).

Peoples and culture: Traditionally the Chechen are divided into several regional tribal communities. These included the MICHIK, QACHALYO, AUKH, and ICHKERI groups, each having their own culture. They lived in the mountains in stone houses with two floors, with the cattle on the ground floor. In some villages (called *auls*) stone towers once used for defending themselves in the Middle Ages still stand.

History: In the sixteenth and seventeenth centuries Chechen began to settle on the plains in the valleys of the Terek, Sungha, and Argun rivers. Under the leadership of Shamil the Chechen fought to keep the Russians out of their territory. However, they were made part of the Russian Empire in 1859. The Chechen-Ingush Autonomous Republic was created in 1936.

In 1944 the autonomous republic came to an end. The people were then sent to Kazakhstan and Siberia. In 1957 most of the Chechen were returned to their land. When the Soviet Union broke up in the early 1990s, the Chechen announced that they were independent of the Russian Federation. A bitter war broke out between the Russians and the Chechens. The country was badly damaged, and many people were killed. After a settlement was reached Chechnya remained within the Russian Federation, at least formally.

Karbulak: The KARBULAK are one of the Chechen tribal communities. There are about 40,000 of them. They moved to the Ottoman Empire and are now spread out among the Middle Eastern countries that came into being after the Ottoman Empire split up. They are known, along with other **ethnic** groups from the North Caucasus, as Circassians. (see CHERKESS)

Economy: The traditional Chechen economy mainly includes cattle-breeding and farming. In the past few years they have begun to work in mining and refining oil.

CHEGMLY A group among the BALKAR in the North Caucasus region of Russia.

CHEHALI The Chehali are a Native North American **ethnic** group that mostly lives in Washington on the Chehali Federal Indian **Reservation**. There are about 1,000 Chehali, who are part of the northwest coast Indian culture. Their language is part of the Salishan family. In the early nineteenth century a smallpox plague hit the CHINOOK people. The many Chinook who did not die from the disease joined the Chehali.

Culture and economy: The Chehali live in wood houses. They make totem poles, which are wooden poles carved with animal and human figures that tell the story of the people's ancestors. The Chehali traditionally make a living by fishing for salmon and sea mammals.

Today the Chehali have a successful salmon-raising business. Many Chehali work in logging.

CHELKAN A group that lives on the southeastern border of the Russian Federation in the Kuznetskii and Ala Tau mountains. The Chelkan are considered to be part of the ALTAI group and speak a Turkic language of the Altai family. They raise cattle and farm.

CHEMWAL A group among the NANDI in Kenya.

CHENCHU The Chenchu are an **ethnic** group of about 18,000 that lives in India, in the Andhra Pradesh, Karnataka, and Orissa regions. They speak the Telugu language, which is a **dialect** of Dravidian.

The Chenchu hunt and gather wild food. They are also expert honey-collectors and bamboo-cutters. They live in thick forests in huts shaped like hives, with walls that are made of branches woven together.

CHENG The Cheng are an **ethnic** group that lives in the southern part of Laos. They are close relatives of the OY people. Their language belongs to the Tibeto-Burman family. Sometimes they grow rice in wet fields. At other times they prepare their land for planting by cutting down and burning any natural growth (slash-and-burn agriculture).

CHEPANG The Chepang are an **ethnic** group of about 25,000 who live in Nepal in the Lothar Khola Region and in valleys of Male Khola in the Mahabharat mountain range. Their language is part of the Tibeto-Burman family.

The Chepang are a Hindu group with Mongolian ancestors. They do not have different social classes like others who live in India. They mainly farm corn and millet. Their houses are made out of tree branches. They trap birds and collect nettles and other items that grow in the forest. Some Chepang also fish and raise animals. The Chepang still use a system of trading services instead of money.

CHERANGANY A group among the MARAKWET in Kenya.

CHERKESS Traditionally the name Cherkess has described three entirely different groups of peoples. First, it is a general name used since the thirteenth century for the Adyghean **ethnic** groups: the ADYGHEANS, the KABARDINIANS, and the CHERKESS of today. The term is also found in traditional Muslim historical and geographical writings. In Turkish they are known as *Cherkas,* in Persian *Charkas,* and Arabic *Sharkasi.* The name of one of the ancient Adyghean tribes, the Kerkete, can also be seen in the name Cherkess.

The second meaning of Cherkess refers to the members of the ethnic groups from the North Caucasus who moved to the Ottoman Empire in 1859–1864. They now live in Turkey and other Middle Eastern countries. There they are known as Circassians. These ethnic groups include most of the western Cherkess tribes, like the ABADZEKH, BJEDUKH, NATUKHAI, SHAPSUG, etc. They also include some of the ABAZIANS, CHECHEN, and INGUSH peoples.

In the third case the Cherkess are an ethnic group that lives in the Karachai-Cherkess Autonomous Region of Russia, in the Greater and Small Zelenchuk river valley. The autonomous region was created in 1922. Its government center is in Cerkessk. The members of this group call themselves Adygheans.

The Cherkess of today are descendants of the Kabardians (the first meaning above) who moved in the first half of the nineteenth century to the upper valley of the Kuban River. They speak the Kabardian language, which is also called Kabardino-Cherkess and High Adyghe. (see also KABARDIANS)

Since the sixteenth century the Cherkess have been Sunni Muslims of the Hanafi school. They are mostly farmers.

CHERO (also called Cheru, Cherwa, and Barahazar) The Chero are an **ethnic** group of about 50,000 that lives in India, in the Palamau, Shahabad, Champaran, Monghyr, Ranchi, Santal Parganas, and Gaya districts of Bihar and West Bengal. They speak a **dialect** of Bihari that belongs to the Indo-Aryan family.

The Chero are a Hindu group. Many live in mud houses. Part of the house is used as a barn for cattle, and another part is used as a storehouse for farm tools and grain.

CHEROKEE The Cherokee are a large Native North American group that lives in northeastern Oklahoma and North Carolina. There are about 50,000 Cherokee in Oklahoma and about 8,000 in North Carolina. They quickly adopted many European-American customs, such as creating their own alphabet and having large farms. Before the Civil War black slaves were used as workers on these farms.

In 1838–1839 all of the Cherokee except one group were moved to the Indian Territory of Oklahoma. This area was 1,200 miles west of their ancient home, and they were forced to walk there. Four thousand people died on the march, which the Cherokee call the Trail of Tears.

Some Cherokee sold their land in Oklahoma at the beginning of the twentieth century. Today they live on the Cherokee Federal **Reservation** in the Great Smoky Mountains of North Carolina and on the Cherokee Federal Trust Area in

Cherokee

Oklahoma. They run a center that displays their Indian culture and that includes a museum and a model of a traditional village. Many Cherokee fought for America during World War II.

CHERU see CHERO.

CHERWA see CHERO.

CHEWA (also called Cewa) The Chewa are a group that lives in the eastern part of Zambia, the Tete region of Mozambique, and the southern part of Malawi. There are about 300,000 Chewa in the three countries.

They speak Nyanja. The ZIMBA are a subgroup of the Chewa.

Religion and culture: Some Chewa are Christians, some are Muslims, and some practice **ancestor worship**. Women are leaders in the Chewa society, and inheritances are passed from mother to daughter. The village leader, called a chief, owns all the land in the village. He gives the land to important people in the village, who divide it up among the villagers. The villagers can sell the produce they have grown, but they cannot sell their land. They have to pay taxes to the people who gave them their land. The Chewa also keep slaves. They are farmers and traders.

History: The Chewa originally came from the Maravi people, who moved before the sixteenth century from the Congo River area to the Lake Malawi area and then to near the Zambezi River. In the eighteenth century the Chewa separated from the Maravi and moved to Mozambique. Some stayed there; others moved farther west. Many members of one group who moved westward under a leader named Mwase of Kasangu, adopted the Muslim religion. Another group, with a leader named Mkanda, moved northward and settled on both sides of the border of Zambia. The European government in control at the time was not able to unite the Chewa under Mkanda.

The Chewa in Mozambique came from the Katanga area in the late fifteenth century. They were very important in the Tete region of Mozambique when that area was fighting for independence. (see also MALAWIANS, MOZAMBICANS, NGONI, NSENGA, ZAMBIANS)

CHE WONG   A group among the SENOI in Malaysia.

CHEYENNE The Cheyenne are a Native North American nation that used to live in Minnesota but were forced to move to the Black Hills of South Dakota. Today there are fewer than 10,000 Cheyenne. Their language belongs to the Algonkian family. There are two major groups of Cheyenne, the Northern and the Southern. The Southern group is close to the ARAPAHO people. Today the Southern Cheyenne and the Arapaho share the same **reservation** in Oklahoma. The Northern Cheyenne are close to the SIOUX Indians who live in the Northern Plains. The two groups fought together at the battle of Little Big Horn,

where the army of General George A. Custer was destroyed.

After this the Northern Cheyenne were forced to move to Oklahoma. However, their two chiefs, Little Wolf and Dull Knife, led them to escape in Montana, where they live today on the Northern Cheyenne Federal Indian Reservation.

CHHAZANG The Chhazang are a group in the northern part of India, in the state of Himachal Pradesh. The Chhazang practice Buddhism. Their culture has been greatly influenced by Tibetan ways.

CHIAPANEC A tiny Native North American people who live in the state of Chiapas in Mexico. (see also MEXICANS)

CHIBCHA The Chibcha are a South American Indian group that lives mostly in Colombia, in the region of Bogotá and Tunja. Before the SPANIARDS arrived in South America, the Chibcha had one of the most modern forms of government and leadership. However, the Spaniards destroyed their government in the sixteenth century. This started the decline of the Chibcha language, although in the eighteenth century almost one million people spoke it.

Women are leaders in Chibcha society, and chiefs are chosen based on who their mother was. However, land is given from father to son. The Chibcha follow their traditional religions and build many small temples in honor of the gods. Their economy is based on farming, crafts, and weaving. They trade products to people from nearby areas for gold. The gold is then used to decorate their temples. They also make it into fancy jewelry and give it to the chiefs to honor them. (see also COLOMBIANS, GUAYMI)

CHICKAHOMINY A small Native North American group that lives in King William County, Virginia, on the Mattapowni State

Reservation. The Chickahominy are part of the Powhatan Confederacy, which is an association of Indian groups.

CHICKASAW The Chickasaw are a Native North American group that used to live in the lower part of Mississippi. Their language is part of the Muskogean family. After signing an agreement with the United States in 1837, the Chickasaw moved to the Indian Territory of Oklahoma. Today many live in the Chickasaw Tribe Federal Trust Area near Ardmore, Oklahoma. There are now about 10,000 Chickasaw. Traditionally they lived in thatched houses.

CHIK BARAIK The Chik Baraik are an **ethnic** group that lives in the states of Bihar and West Bengal, India. In 1981 there were 53,000 of them.

The Chik Baraik economy is based on the forest. They traditionally work at weaving. They also hunt and look for food in their area. Their houses are usually spread out, with two or three families living in each.

CHIL see KIL.

CHILAPA A group among the JIVARO of northern Ecuador.

CHILCOTIN (also called Tsilkotin) The Chilcotin are a Native North American group that lives in Canada, in the south-central part of British Columbia. Today there are about 1,700 of them. Their language is part of the Athpaskan family. Many Chilcotin work outside of the **reservation**. However, they also make money by traditional hunting and fishing.

CHILEANS The Chileans are the people living in the South American country of Chile. There are 15 million of them. They are mostly white, even though they have married into Indian groups like the ARAUCANIANS since the SPANIARDS came to the area in the sixteenth century. Spanish is spoken. However, some groups of newcomers to the country maintain the languages of their homelands.

Ninety percent of Chileans live in the central valley of Chile, which is a good piece of land for farming between the Andean Mountains and the coast. The largest number of Chileans who live outside the country is in Argentina. The main group of workers in Patagonia, Argentina, was Chilean. They were kicked out of Argentina in the 1970s because there was fighting between Argentina and Chile. This fighting almost led to war in 1978. Other large groups of Chileans live in the poorer areas of Buenos Aires, Argentina.

History: During the years when Spain ruled the area (from the sixteenth to nineteenth centuries) Chile was hard to reach. This isolation led to the development of a special Chilean culture. Several events made the Chileans feel strongly about having their own independent country: the war of independence of 1810–1818; the creation of a government with total control in 1833; the war from 1836 to 1839 against the joint armies of Peru and Bolivia; and the Pacific War between Bolivia, Chile, and Peru from 1879 to 1883. In the last two wars Chile took over the areas of Atacama and Tarapaca, which had important and valuable minerals called nitrites. These resources made the Chileans think they could be free and independent.

Europeans: Until the midnineteenth century newcomers to Chile were mostly from Spain, including BASQUES, CASTILIANS, and ANDALUSIANS. After 1848 Germans were also urged to settle in Chile. Many Germans arrived in the Valdivia and Llanquihue regions in the southern part of the country. During the nineteenth and the beginning of the twentieth centuries other Europeans also began to settle in Chile: ITALIANS, FRENCH, BRITISH, SWISS, AUSTRIANS, CROATIANS, JEWS, and ARABS. Because

Top: Chileans in a tavern

Bottom: Chilean mussel-vendors

the government decided that these Europeans could enter the country, they were not seen as outsiders pushing their way in, and they blended in easily.

Many reasons contributed to the ability of **ethnic** groups in Chile to get along with one another. Each ethnic group was allowed and encouraged to practice its traditions. Since the Chileans believed in their right to have their own country, they also believed that others should have rights. The Chileans had a democratic tradition of representation for the opinions of all the people in the government. There were large divisions between social classes in Chile. Because there were such obvious differences between classes, people paid less attention to the differences between ethnic groups.

Indians: The Indians of Chile make up about two percent of the population. They are mostly ARAUCANIANS. They speak their own Mapuche language and Spanish. They live in the central southern part of Chile, between the Biobio and Tolten rivers.

Religion: About 90 percent of Chileans are Roman Catholics. But openness and a law passed in 1925 about the separation between government and religion have allowed different types of people to practice their own beliefs. A tenth of Chileans have adopted different forms of Protestantism. There are also about 10,000 Jews in Chile. Not long ago some Muslims built a mosque, their house of worship, in Santiago.

Society and culture: Since the Europeans arrived, Chileans have been divided into richer and poorer social classes. The Chileans use the idea of the *roto,* which means "the broken one," to symbolize the typical person. The *roto* is poor, works hard, has a good sense of humor, and likes drinking wine.

More than 83 percent of Chileans live in cities. The rest live in rural areas. *Huasos* are the traditional Chilean cowboys. They are famous for their ability to handle horses and show this skill in Chilean rodeos. However, traditional customs are dying out, and Chileans are becoming more modern. A middle class (which is a modern idea) quickly developed after the 1930s. It became an important part of Chile's government and society.

Because there was so large a gap between the rich and the poor in Chile, there was a time of crisis in politics when the country split into opposing political groups. Divisions were so extreme that Chile was terribly weakened. Soon the Chilean economy and democracy were destroyed, and the army was able to take control of the government. In the 1990s the government began to bring back democracy, which gave the people more of a say in how the country is run. (see also ARAUCANIANS)

CHIMBA   A group among the HERERO in Angola.

CHIMBU (also called Simbu) The Chimbu are an **ethnic** group that lives in the mountains in the central part of Papua New Guinea. There are more than 80,000 Chimbu. They speak a local language. The Chimbu do not have an organized religion or priests. Instead, their beliefs are based on **ancestor worship**. The Chimbu economy relies on growing different fruits and vegetables, like the sweet potato, and on farming coffee.

CHIN see BURMANS.

CHINESE   There are over 1.2 billion people living in China—the country with the world's largest population. China has 56 major **ethnic** groups. The largest group is the Han, who are often just called "the Chinese." However, this is not really an accurate name; it is more correct to call them HAN CHINESE. The Han Chinese make up 92 percent of the Chinese population. Their culture is the strongest and most widespread in China.

The Han Chinese live all over China. There are also large Han Chinese communities in many other Asian countries: Thailand, Malaysia, Indonesia, Singapore, Hong Kong, Vietnam, Burma, the Philippines, and Cambodia. In fact, in Singapore and Hong Kong, the populations are mostly Han Chinese. There are Han Chinese living in countries outside of Asia, too. Most groups that live outside of China are descendants of farmers and fisherman who lived in China's coastal areas. The largest number of Han Chinese who moved to other countries in Southeast Asia left in the 1920s.

spoken **dialect**, but for many. This has greatly helped maintain a united Chinese culture. Although different groups in China may speak different dialects, all use the same written language to represent the same ideas. Even though it has changed a lot over hundreds of years, Han Chinese is still used today.

There are huge differences between the languages of different Chinese ethnic groups. They speak very different dialects of Han Chinese, and many groups cannot understand the

A Chinese noodle-maker

Language: The Han Chinese language is a member of the Sino-Tibetan family. It is written as a picture language. Its modern written form comes from as far back as 2,000 B.C. Even older forms have been found written on bronze, stone, bone, and tortoise shells that are at least 3,500 to 4,000 years old. The pictures are a written language *only;* they are used not for just one

languages of others. The differences are almost as great as those between different European languages. There are seven main dialect groups: Mandarin, which is the largest and spoken by about 70 percent of Han Chinese; Wu, which is spoken in Shanghai and the nearby areas; Gan, also called Kan; Xiang, also called Hsiang; Yue, which is also known as Cantonese; Kejia, also called Hakka; and Min. The official language of China is called Putonghua, which means "common language" or "standard Chinese." Putonghua comes from the Beijing dialect of northern Mandarin. Most Han Chinese speak and understand Putonghua, as do smaller groups.

Religion and culture: The Han Chinese follow a mixture of beliefs and religions. The most popular are Taoism and Confucianism, which were both developed in China, and Buddhism. However, **ancestor worship** is also an important practice.

small, active, and soft-spoken. Northern Mandarins are often described as proud, honest, and direct. People in the northwest are known to be simple, traditional, and careful with their money. Southerners, especially from Shanghai and areas surrounding that city, are thought to be practical and smart. The Cantonese are known as loyal to family, hardworking, excited to find new ideas, and unwilling to give up. Just as there are different **dialects** from different areas, there are also different types of music, art, and food. There

Traditional Chinese river boats near Lanchow in central China

The Han Chinese are really one large group with the same traditions, culture, and written language. But because they live all over such a huge country with different ways, they do not share the same habits or lifestyles. They often divide themselves up based on where they are from. For example, people usually think of the northern Han Chinese as tall and strong, while southerners tend to be

are also large differences in various regions in the level of wealth and development, in standards of living, education, and so on. The areas near the coast are usually more modern and have more industry than the regions in the center of the country. Also, people in the south tend to be richer, more successful, and more educated than those in the northwest parts of China.

Top: A Chinese religious ceremony

Bottom: Chinese women picking tea leaves

Top: A Zhuang woman with a yoke for carrying goods from the market
Bottom: Chinese practicing Tai Chi in the middle of a Shanghai street

History: The history of the Han Chinese is very complicated. Experts believe that they originally came from the farming tribes that lived in the valleys of the Yellow and Yangtze rivers. These tribes created a new culture during the Stone Age between 4,000 and 5,000 years ago.

China was first joined together under the rule of the Qin dynasty in 221–207 B.C. The Han Chinese appeared during the Han dynasty, which held power from 206 B.C. to 220 A.D. At first the people settled in the regions of the Yellow and Wei rivers. These areas are known as "the cradle of Chinese civilization." Later, some moved further east and then to the south and southwest. When the Han Chinese settled in new places, they usually forced the different ethnic groups already living there to join with them. Under the Tang dynasty, which ruled from 618 to 907, China became the cultural and economic center of Asia. Industry and trade were very successful. China also fought and won several wars in Central Asia and Korea.

The Han Chinese ruled China for more years than any other group. However, two groups from outside China took control at different times. These were the Yuan group from Mongolia, which ruled from 1271 to 1368, and the Manchurian Qing, which ruled China from 1644 to 1911. The MANCHU people adopted Chinese culture, laws, and the Chinese style of government.

The Manchus were overthrown in the early part of the twentieth century. For almost 40 years afterward the Han Chinese fought over who would take power. In 1949 the Communists took control under the leadership of Mao Zedong. They tried to make China a modern industrial country very quickly. They also tried to change the way the society worked. There was an economic crisis in the early 1960s. This forced the Communists to take steps backward until 1965 and to fix what they had changed. In that year Mao started a movement called the Cultural Revolution. Its goal was to attack government workers, the educated, scientists, and any people or groups who had connections with countries outside China. It also included forcing about 60 million younger people, who were mostly between the ages of 16 and 30, to resettle. They were moved away from the areas where most people lived for several reasons: to work in farming; to take back land in areas that were hard to reach; to settle areas on the Chinese border; to increase the Han Chinese population in regions that were not mostly Han Chinese; to make the big cities less crowded and poor; and to take businesses with them to new regions. The Communists wanted to make the Han Chinese the largest and most important ethnic group all over China. However, they did not become the main part of the population in some areas. There were few in the northern and western parts of the country.

Peoples: Besides the Han Chinese there are China 55 smaller ethnic groups. The largest of those groups is the ZHUANG, a people who practice the Buddhist religion, are related to the DAI people, and live in Guangxi, Yunnan, and Guangdong provinces. Other large groups are: the HUI, who speak Han Chinese, are Muslims, and live mainly in Ningxia, Gansu, Henan, and Hebe provinces; the UIGUR, who are Turkic Muslims and live in Xinjiang Province; the YI, who practice Buddhism, are related to the TIBETANS, and live in Yunnan, Sichuan, and Guizhou provinces; and the MIAO, who live in Guizhou, Hunan, Yunnan, and Guangxi provinces. Tibetans live mainly in Tibet (which was invaded and conquered by China in 1950), Qinghai, and Sichuan provinces.

There are several other ethnic groups that have sizable populations. These include: the MONGOLS, MANCHU, BUYI, KOREANS, DONG, YAO, BAI, and KAZAKHS. Besides them China also has small communities like the DAUR, LAHU, LI, LISU, NAXI, SALAR, SHE, SHUI, SIBO, DAI, TU, and WA.

All of these groups, which are smaller than the Han, used to be allowed by the government to have as many children as they wanted. However, in 1982 China's rulers decided that they needed to cut the population even more, so they also put restrictions on the smaller groups. But while the Han were only allowed one child per family, the other groups were allowed as many as four children per family.

Economy: About 75 percent of the Han Chinese are still farmers. However, more and more have began working in trade and business. They also work at many types of crafts.

In the 1970s China became friendlier with the countries of the West, partly because both China and the Western countries did not trust the Soviet Union. This pushed China to develop more modern industry, farming, army, science, and technology.

However, modernizing has only taken place in the economy. China is still ruled by a Communist government. Elderly rulers have total control over the people. In 1989 the government violently put down a peaceful rally of students who were demonstrating for democracy in Tianenman Square in China's capital of Beijing. The Western countries that China trades with strongly protested China's behavior. Some countries banned trade with China. However, because trading with China earns those countries so much money, most quickly removed their bans.

In the 1990s China's economy has been developing very quickly as a result of the country being more open to the world market. Private ownership of businesses has also been encouraged, and many new factories have been opened. China is exporting its products to the outside world more and more. (see also THAI)

CHINGATHAN A small **ethnic** group that lives in the southern part of India, in the state of Kerala's northern region. They mainly make a living by gathering wild honey.

CHING-PO see SINGHPO.

CHINOOK The Chinook are a small Native North American group of a few hundred that used to be one of the largest groups in the Pacific northwest area. Most of the tribe died in a smallpox plague in the 1830s. The rest joined the CHEHALI group, who now live on the Federal Indian **Reservation** in Washington.

Chinook

CHIPEWYAN The Chipewyan are a Native North American group of about 5,000 that lives in northern Canada, in the Mackenzie River Delta, the Northwest Territories, and in the northern part of Alberta. Their language is part of the Athapaskan family. Because of where they live, the Chipewyan act as middlemen between the INUIT who live to the north and the Woodland CREE who live to the south. The number of Chipewyan who cannot find jobs is one of the highest in Canada. Many Chipewyan try to hold on to their traditional practices of hunting and trapping animals.

CHIPPEWA (also called Ojibway) The Chippewa are one of the largest Native North American peoples. There are 100,000 Chippewa in Canada and 70,000 in the United States. They live in many communities across Quebec, Ontario, Manitoba, and Saskatchewan in Canada and in Minnesota, Wisconsin, and North Dakota. Their language, Ojibway, is part of the Algonkian family and is divided into several **dialects**.

Traditionally the Chippewa are hunters who also gather wild food in their area. Some also grow corn and wild rice. They once lived in houses called wigwams, which are tents covered by birch bark. The Chippewa were also famous for their birch bark canoes.

The Chippewa were strong fighters. They were allies of the BRITISH in their wars against the United States. In 1812 the Chippewa destroyed the city of Detroit. Today the Chippewa are fighting over land ownership and fishing rights with the United States government and the state government of Wisconsin. Violence broke out over this in 1989 and 1990.

CHIQUITO The Chiquito are a South American Indian people numbering about 43,000 who live in the lowlands of Bolivia. They speak a language in the Gê family. They farm, mainly a starchy vegetable called sweet manioc, corn, pineapples, sweet potatoes, beans, cotton, and peppers. They also hunt, fish, and gather wild food.

They were originally part of the GUARANI people who live in Paraguay. The Chiquito moved to where they now live when the PORTUGUESE came to Brazil and took control.

CHIRICAHUA A group among the APACHE.

CHIRIGUANOS The Chiriguanos are an **ethnic** group of South American Indians who live in Bolivia, in the Chiquisaca and Tarija regions, as well as in nearby areas in Argentina and Paraguay. They number over 30,000. When

Chiriguanos

Europeans came to South America, there were 200,000 Chiriguanos. Many Chiriguanos died or moved away because the Europeans violently forced cattle-farming into the Chiriguanos' corn-growing farmlands. In 1875 and 1892 the Europeans sent the Chiriguanos to Argentina to work on cattle farms. Some ran away to churches and **missionary** settlements.

The Chaco war of 1932–1935 between Bolivia and Paraguay also caused many Chiriguanos to leave their homes. They were caught in the middle of the war, so they fled to Argentina or Paraguay.

CHIRIMA An **ethnic** group that lives in Mozambique.

CHIRUMBA A group among the SHONA in southern Africa.

CHISHINGA The Chishinga are a group that lives in Zambia, in the region north of Lake Bangweulu. There are about 85,000 of them. They speak Bemba. They have kept their traditional religion, but some are Christian. During the nineteenth century the Chishinga made iron. The family line and inheritances pass

Chisinga

from the mother, rather than the father, to children. The Chishinga originally come from the LUBA Empire in southeast Congo (Zaire). They were conquered by the BEMBA group in the early 1890s.

CHITIMACHA   The Chitimacha are a Native North American group that used to live in Mississippi. They now live on the Chitimacha Federal Indian **Reservation** in southern Louisiana. There are several hundred Chitimacha, but none left who speak their native language.

CHITRALI   A small group that lives in the mountainous areas in the northern part of Pakistan. The Chitrali are Sunni Muslims. They live in the valleys and herd animals.

CHITRARI   see KHO.

CHIZEZURU   see ZEZURU.

CHOCTAW   The Choctaw are a large Native North American group that used to live in the southeast part of the Mississippi Valley. Today there are about 40,000 of them. Six thousand still live on their homeland on the Choctaw Federal Indian Reservation in Neshoba County, Mississippi. Most of the rest live in the Choctaw Federal Trust Area in Pushmataha and Latimer counties in Oklahoma.

The Choctaw traditionally lived by fishing and growing corn. They were one of the first Native American groups to move to Oklahoma. In their language, which is part of the Muskogean family, the word Oklahoma means "Red Men."

The Choctaw have maintained their own language more than many other Native American groups. More than 1,000 work at the car building factory on the Mississippi reservation. The factory is owned and run by Choctaw.

CHOISEUL ISLANDERS   The Choiseul Islanders are an **ethnic** group of about 10,000 that lives in the southwest part of the Pacific Ocean, in the Solomon Islands. Their main area is Choiseul Island. They speak four local **dialects** that are part of the Malayo-Polynesian family.

Choctaw

They prepare their land for farming by cutting down and burning any natural growth (slash-and-burn agriculture). When their fields become worn out, they create new ones nearby. Their main crop is taro. The traditional beliefs of the Islanders have been replaced by Christianity.

CHOKOSSI (call themselves Anufo) The Chokossi are an **ethnic** group of about 100,000 that lives in the Sansanne-Mango and Dpaong areas of Togo, and in Ghana and Benin. There are about 45,000 Chokossi in Togo and 55,000 in Ghana. They speak Anufo, which is a **dialect** in the Kwa group of the Niger-Congo family. They practice mostly their traditional religion, but some are Muslims. Different groups of Chokossi are given very different levels of respect and privileges in their society.

Before Europeans came to Africa, a Chokossi kingdom held power over the nearby areas of MOBA, GURMA, and GUANG. The Chokossi capital was in Sansanne-Mango. In Togo the Chokossi fought for some time against the Germans who had come to Africa. However, after a while they helped the Germans take over the rest of the country. Even though there are not many Chokossi in Togo, quite a few of them play a role in the government.

Chokossi

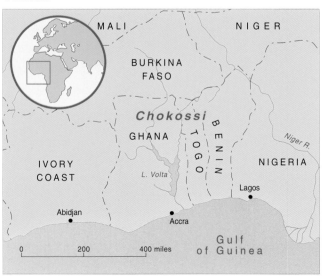

CHOKWE (also called Tshokwe) The Chokwe are a people of over one million who live in the eastern part of Angola, in the northwest part of Zambia, and in the southern part of the Shaba (Katanga) Region in Congo (Zaire). There are about 450,000 Chokwe in Angola, 50,000 in Zambia, and 500,000 in Congo (Zaire). Their language is part of the Bantu group in the Niger-Congo family. They used to be a society of sometimes **nomads** that was ruled by the LUNDA group for hundreds of years. The family line and inheritances pass from mother, rather than father, to children. The Chokwe rebelled against the Lunda in the nineteenth century. They were independent for the 10 years between 1885 and 1895. Later the entire country fell under Belgian rule and was known as the Belgian Congo.

After Congo (Zaire) gained independence in 1960, people in the Katanga Region (now called Shaba) also wanted to have their own country, separate from Congo (Zaire). This was called the "Katanga crisis." At that time the Chokwe joined with the LUBA to organize a political party called Bulabakat, which was against Katanga separating from Congo (Zaire). Katanga, after a bitter war, remained within Congo (Zaire). Later, the Chokwe became angry at the government for taking advantage of Katanga's natural resources without giving anything back. (see also CONGOLESE [CONGO (ZAIRE)])

CHONG The Chong are an **ethnic** group that lives mainly in the region along the southern border of Cambodia and Thailand. There are about 5,000 of them. They speak a Mon-Khmer language. Experts think that the Chong used to live in a much larger area. However, they have since been absorbed into KHMER society. Many believe that the SAOCH group are descendants of the Chong who would not allow themselves to be taken into Khmer society.

CHONO The Chono are a South American Indian people who live in Chile, along the coast and in Tierra del Fuego, as well as on islands off of those regions. The Chono are sometimes **nomadic**. They live by collecting mussels and shellfish, fishing, and hunting seals and porpoises.

CHONTAL The Chontal are a small **ethnic** group that lives in Mexico in the southernmost parts of the state of Oaxaca. The Chontal's ancestors, from the time before Columbus came to America, were less advanced and powerful than their ZAPOTEC neighbors.

The Chontal are divided into two groups, the Highland and the Lowland groups. The Highland Chontal live in an area that is harder to reach. Their language belongs to the Hokan family and is somewhat similar to Aztec. But because there are no written records, it is not known if the Chontal were conquered by the Aztecs or whether the Aztecs only influenced the Chontal language. Like many other native groups in the southern part of Mexico, the Chontal are not really part of Mexican society. Some have been taught to read and write Spanish by government teachers in rural areas. However, most speak Chontal at home.

Language: The Chontal have taken many aspects of Mexican culture and the Spanish language into their everyday life. Their language has so much Spanish in it that it is hard to say what is Spanish and what is Chontal. Older people speak real Chontal. But younger people find that they cannot speak either language by itself.

Religion: The Chontal have two forms of religious practices. Publicly they are Roman Catholics; in private they practice their traditional religion. Since Catholicism was celebrated in Latin and then in Spanish, the Chontal did not always understand it. For example, because the sun used to be one of their most important gods, today they think of the sun as similar to Jesus. They compare the moon to the Virgin Mary.

Chontal

They practice their traditional customs at home or in woodland caves in an attempt to please the devil. (see also MAYA, MEXICANS)

CHONYI A group among the MIJIKENDA in eastern Kenya.

CHOPI The Chopi are a people numbering about 800,000 who live in Mozambique, along the southern coasts. They speak a Bantu language. Some Chopi still practice traditional religions; many others are Christians and go to Methodist and Catholic schools.

The PORTUGUESE arrived in their present region in 1870. The Chopi had hoped that the Portuguese would help them against the SHANGAAN group. At first the Chopi had a good relationship with the Portuguese, but later they protested Portuguese control.

The Chopi are famous for their special musical instruments. They wrote many songs condemning the Portuguese rulers. (see also MOZAMBICANS)

CHOROTE A tribe of the MATACO-MATAGUAYO in Argentina.

CHOROTEGA A Native Central American group that lives in Costa Rica and El Salvador.

CHORTI A group among the MAYA in Guatemala.

CHRAU An **ethnic** group that lives in the hilly southern part of Vietnam, in the region around Ho Chi Minh City (previously Saigon). There are about 15,000 of them. Their language is in the Mon-Khmer family. Their name means "hill dwellers."

CHRU see CHURU.

CHUABO (also called Acwabo and Cwabo) The Chuabo are a people that numbers about 800,000. They live in Mozambique, on the left bank of the lower part of the Zambezi River valley. They speak a Bantu language. The first Chaubo were part of the local Maravi Empire. Some are Christians or Muslims, but most follow their traditional religion.

CHUANG see ZHUANG.

CHUKA A group among the MERU in central Kenya.

CHUKCHANSI (also called Yokuts) A small Native North American group that today lives in San Joaquin Valley, California.

CHUKCHI The Chukchi are an **ethnic** group that lives on the Chukchi Peninsula in northeastern Siberia, in the most northern part of Asia. There are about 17,000 of them, making up about 15 percent of the population of the Chukchi District of northeast Russia. In 1926, 70 percent of the Chukchi were nomads. Today most live in

Chukchi

permanent settlements, and only some are still **seminomads**.

Their language, Chuko, is closely related to the Koryak and Helmen languages, but people speaking one of these languages do not necessarily understand one another. Since 1831 Chukchi has been written in the Cyrillic alphabet (used for Russian).

The Chukchi are divided into two groups. The CHAVCHU are reindeer-herders who are nomads and seminomads. The AN'KALYN are fishing people and fur-trappers who live along the coast. They An'kalyn also work in mining. Even though the Russians tried to force the Chukchi to abandon their traditional rituals, the people still practice them. Their rituals are based on belief in spirits.

CHULIKATTA see MISHMI.

CHULUPI A tribe of the MATACO-MATAGUAYO in Argentina.

CHUMASH The Chumash are a Native North American group on the southern California coast. There are about 300 of them. When the Spanish arrived in their area in the eighteenth century, there were more than 20,000. They quickly adopted Spanish farming practices. Today members of the Chumash live on the Santa Ynez Federal **Reservation** in Santa Barbara, California.

CHUNG-CHIA see BUYI.

CHURAHI A Hindu people who live in India, in the Chamba District of the northern state of Himachal Pradesh.

CHURU (also called Chru) The Churu are a Malayo-Polynesian group that lives in the mountains of the southern part of Vietnam. There are about 10,000 of them. Their language is part of the Malayo-Polynesian family and is similar to the language of the CHAM. The Churu were the only **ethnic** group living in the mountains of Vietnam to create their own alphabet before the Europeans arrived in the area. It is based on an Indian alphabet.

CHUTIA (also called Dibongiya) The Chutia are a people who live in India, in the western area of the state of Assam. They speak a language that is part of the Sino-Tibetan family. The Chutia used to be the main **ethnic** group in the region. However, they have become less important in the past few years.

CHUTIYA An **ethnic** group that lives in the eastern part of India, in the states of Nagaland, Arunachal Pradesh, and Assam.

CHUTY A group among the JARAI in south-central Vietnam.

CHUUK ISLANDERS (also called Chuukese and Trukese) The Chuuk Islanders are a people numbering about 50,000 who live on the Chuuk Islands (which used to be called the Truk Islands). This is a group of 14 main volcanic islands scattered throughout a 40 mile-wide body of water in the center of the Caroline Islands.

History: At the beginning of the twentieth century the islands were ruled by Germany. In 1920 the JAPANESE took control, and the United States took over in 1945. Today the island group is a member of the Federated States of Micronesia, which is associated with the United States.

Language and culture: The Chuuk Islanders' language is part of the Malayo-Polynesian family. There are several family groups (clans) in the islands' society. The family line and inheritances pass from mother, rather than father, to children. The decision about who can marry whom is based on clans. The Chuuk Islanders are mainly Roman Catholic. They grow their own food; their main crop is breadfruit. They produce and sell copra, a dried coconut product that is used as an oily ingredient in processed food. They also fish.

CHUUKESE see CHUUK ISLANDERS.

CHUVASH The Chuvash are a people who live in different areas in the Russian Federation, but mainly in Chuvashia, the former Chuvash Autonomous Republic. There are about 1.8 million Chuvash in the Russian Federation. Others live in the nearby Tatar and Bashkir regions. Some Chuvash moved to Siberia during the nineteenth and twentieth centuries.

Language: The Chuvash language belongs to the Turkic family. It is not necessarily understood by speakers of other Turkic languages. The Chuvash have both European and MONGOLIAN ancestors. They are divided into two groups according to which **dialect** they speak: Viryal

(Upper) and Anatri (Lower) Chuvash. The Anatri dialect was used in the 1870s to create a written language that employs the Cyrillic alphabet (used for Russian).

History: The Chuvash claim that they originally come from the Volga-Bulgars. A group called the TATARS also claims they come from the Volga-Bulgars. There are experts who agree and disagree with each group. Writings about the Chuvash first appear in traditional records from the fifteenth century, when they were ruled by the Tatars.

In 1551 the Chuvash lands were taken by the RUSSIANS. In the first half of the eighteenth century the Chuvash were forced to become Russian Orthodox Christians and abandon their own religious practices.

Culture: The traditional jobs of the Chuvash were farming and raising cattle. Until the Russian

Chuvash

Revolution of 1917 they were spread out in rural areas and had a traditional lifestyle. When the Soviets took control, and especially since World War II, many Chuvash found industrial work in the cities. Some are still involved in their traditional crafts and activities: choir singing, embroidery, special weaving, and wood carving.

CHYSH-KIZHI see SHORS.

CIBECUE A group among the APACHE in the southwestern United States.

CIL A group among the MNONG in Vietnam.

CINTA LARGA A tiny South American Indian group that lives in central-west Brazil, in the state of Mato Grosso. There are fewer than 1,000 Cinta Larga, and they have very little contact with others. Their name was given to them because of the long ribbons that they wear around their waists. They are hunters, fishing people, and gatherers of fruit.

CIRCASSIANS see ABAZIANS, CHERKESS, CHECHEN.

COCAMA The Cocama are a South American Indian group that lives mostly in Peru with a few across the border in Brazil in the area around the upper Amazon River. In Peru the Cocama speak Spanish and those in Brazil speak Portuguese. They number about 15,000. They speak the Tupi-Guarani language, which is part of the Tupi family. There are very few speakers of the native language left.

COCHINESE see VIETNAMESE.

COCOPAH A small Native North American nation of about 5,000. Many Cocopah live in the southern part of California, on the Cocopah Federal Indian **Reservation** in Yuma County.

Others are found across the border in Mexico and in Baja, California.

COFÁN The Cofán are a South American Indian group of about 1,200 who live in the eastern part of Ecuador and across the border in Colombia. They live in several villages at the headwaters of the Aguarico and San Miguel rivers. They speak their own language, which is part of the Chibchan family. Even though the Cofán have adopted Roman Catholicism and some of the modern customs of the people around them, they also use traditional magical practices to settle arguments and cure illnesses.

A Cofán woman

COLLAGUA A group among the AYMARA in western South America.

COLLAHUAYA A group among the AYMARA in western South America.

COLOMBIANS The Colombians live in Colombia, a country in the northwest part of South America, between the Caribbean Sea and the Pacific Ocean. There are 37 million of them. Before the Spanish arrived in 1512, the CHIBCHA Indians, who lived in the western mountain regions, were the main **ethnic** group in the area. The population of Colombia today is made up of

Cofán men

Top: Colombians in a village market

Bottom: Colombian father and daughter working with a small sugarcane press

COLOMBIANS AND THE ENVIRONMENT

In the central Colombian region of Cauca there are people from many different **ethnic** groups and social classes. They live and farm their fields close together, but a view from the air will make one thing clear: they are not all the same.

In the Cauca region landowners have cut and burned the natural growth in their fields in order to plant potatoes and raise cows for milk. This is true for farmers of European origin in the area: they believe that the natural growth is just in the way and should be destroyed.

The Indian groups that live in the area treat their land rather differently because they believe that land plays an important part in maintaining balance in the world. They think that the world is divided in two parts: the Upper World that belongs to man, and the Lower World, which belongs to the ancient spirits. However, the spirits also inhabit parts of the Upper World as well, and they are believed to cause sickness and bad luck. The Indian groups believe that life and health are only possible when there is balance between man and the spirits, and that illness happens when nature is out of balance. Therefore Indian farmers make fields and pastures, but they also try to leave nature alone whenever possible. As a result, there are strict rules about farming, and their land preserves forests, mountains, and outcrops.

The Indians in the Cauca region believe that mountains, valleys, seas, and rivers are areas where the spirits are very powerful, and so they leave these spots alone. However, in the low flatland water

An Indian woman with reed mats to be sold in the market in the Cauca region

is absorbed by the ground, making excellent land for farming.

The Caucas have medicine men who are able to contact the Lower World and are the only people who can communicate with the spirits. In order to do his work, the medicine man needs such things as plants from where spirits are supposed to live, like the forest or the slope of a mountain. The best medicines are taken from wild animals such as the puma, deer, bear, or tapir.

It is clear what part of this Cauca land is farmed and what cannot be cultivated

Leading members of the Cauca Indian council talk about an issue

government of Colombia has declared some of these areas protected as well, but many Indians oppose the idea. They are afraid that even though the plants and animals will be more protected than before, tourists will come and destroy their way of life. The white man may not understand the Indians of Colombia, but for the Cauca the land is much more than a place to plant crops. For them the land is life itself, and disturbing the relationship between farmland and wilderness would be harmful both to the land and the people.

Pottery is made in the Cauca region using ancient methods. It is then sold at the market

The Cauca also think that their behavior in daily life can affect the balance of nature. Therefore there are rules to control birth, childhood, puberty, sexuality, menstruation, and death—virtually all areas of life.

Since ancient times the Cauca have only allowed certain people to travel to the high plateau of the Central Mountains. Even those allowed to go there could bring back only animals and plants that were believed to cure people. The

descendants of marriages between Indians, SPANIARDS, and African newcomers. Experts estimate that almost half of the population is made up of European-Indian people, while one-fifth have a European-African heritage.

Language and religion: Most Colombians speak Spanish. There are also several native languages that are spoken by important ethnic groups such as: the AYMARA, ARAWAK, CHIBCHA, CARIB, QUECHUA, TUPI-GUARANI, and YURUMANGUI. Most Colombians are Roman Catholics.

Regions: Since Colombia is the only country in Latin America with both Caribbean and Pacific coastlines, it has one of the world's most mixed environments. This includes the high Andes Mountains and the low, tropical area around the Amazon River. Colombia has many different types of plants and animals. It also has plentiful minerals, and the government controls their use. There are also some natural fuel resources in Colombia. However, only five percent of the land in Colombia (mostly in valleys in the mountainous regions) is good for farming, and only 30 percent is very good for animals to graze on. Since there is not much land for farming, and because Colombia has some of the highest birthrates and population growth rates in Latin America, many more Colombians live in cities than in rural areas. In the late 1950s about two-thirds of Colombians lived in rural regions, while in the late 1980s almost two-thirds lived in cities. Many people who move to the cities live in disorganized areas called *barrios populares.*

Economy: Colombians farm several main crops, including beans, bananas, cassava, corn, potatoes, and rice. They also grow tobacco for use in Colombia. Coffee is Colombia's best-known legal crop raised for selling outside of the country; however, an illegal crop called coca is turned into the drug cocaine. Coca makes twice the amount of money that coffee does. Indians who live in the Andes Mountains make

coca into a strong tea. Other businesses that are important in Colombia are forestry and manufacturing. Water from Colombia's rivers is turned into hydroelectric power, which runs 75 percent of the factories.

Even though Colombians produce a lot of transportation equipment, they themselves do not have a very efficient transportation system, especially in rural areas. Fewer than one-third of the roads in Colombia are paved. There are many Colombians who know how to read and write, but there are still not enough educated people to work in certain important fields such as medicine. Because of this, several diseases are still a problem in Colombia.

History: The Spanish took control of the area in 1525. The region of Santa Fe de Bogota became part of the kingdom of Peru in 1559. It was transferred to the kingdom of New Granada

A Colombian farmer with his horse near the village market

in 1740. New Granada was created by combining the areas that are now called Colombia, Ecuador, and Venezuela. The Creoles, Europeans who were born in South America, were afraid that they would lose their wealth if the Spanish stayed in control. They rebelled against the Spanish in 1781 in an uprising called the Comunero Revolt. The area won its freedom in 1821, and New Granada became the Republic of Gran Colombia, which lasted until 1830.

In the second half of the nineteenth century and the beginning of the twentieth century there was a great deal of conflict between the Liberal and Conservative political parties. There has been much violence in Colombia in the past few years. It has been caused both by politics and by Colombia's international drug business, which is based in the city of Medellin.

COLVILLE

COLVILLE (also called Wenatch) The Colville are a small Native North American group. Most of the 500 Colville are found today on the Colville **Reservation** in north-central Washington. They speak a Salishan language. The Colville are related to the LILLOOET group and the COMOX group in British Columbia, Canada.

COMANCHE

COMANCHE The Comanche are a Native North American group that used to live on the northern plains of Texas. Their language is part of the Uto-Aztecan family.

They were famous for being the best horsemen and soldiers among the Plains Indians. In the eighteenth and nineteenth centuries they were one of the largest and strongest tribes among the southern Plains Indians. For 200 years they were able to prevent the SPANIARDS and MEXICANS from moving into their territory.

In 1874 the Comanche were moved from their land to a **reservation** in the Oklahoma Territory. During the nineteenth century the number of Comanche steeply declined. Today there are only

Comanche

about 4,000. Many live on the Comanche Tribe's Federal Trust Area in Oklahoma.

COMECHINGON AND SANAVIRON

COMECHINGON AND SANAVIRON The small numbers of people who are left from a native group that used to live in what is now Cordoba, Argentina.

COMORANS

COMORANS The Comorans are a people who live in the tiny Republic of the Comoros. It is made up of several islands in the Mozambique Channel between the island of Madagascar and the mainland of Africa. There are about 580,000 Comorans. They originally come from a combination of African, ARAB, and MALAGASY ancestors. Their language is Comorian, which is a combination of Swahili and Arabic; it is written in Arabic script. Most Comorans are Sunni Muslims, but there is also a small Christian community. It is made up of those left from the many people who became Christians under the FRENCH, who ruled the area at one time. About 80 percent of Comorans are farmers.

In 1974 the Comorans had a countrywide vote in which they decided to become independent of France. Only one group, the people who lived on the southernmost island of Mayotte, voted to remain part of France. Independence was declared for all the islands in 1975. However, Mayotte is still ruled by France.

COMOX The Comox are a Native North American group. There are about 500 of them living in the southwestern part of British Columbia, Canada, as well as on Vancouver and Comox islands. The Comox traditionally made a living by salmon fishing. Some still use the group's traditional fishing spots. (see also COLVILLE)

CONGOLESE (Congo [Zaire]) The Congolese are the people of Congo, which used to be known as Zaire. It is the second largest country in Africa, found in the center of the continent.

Peoples and regions: Experts estimate that 47 million people live in Congo (Zaire). They include many **ethnic** groups that live in different parts of the country. The KONGO, who live in the southwest, are divided between Congo (Zaire), the Republic of Congo, and Angola; the ZANDE, in the northeast, live in Congo (Zaire) and Sudan; the CHOKWE, in the southwest, are found in Congo (Zaire) and Angola; the BEMBA, in the southeast, live in Congo (Zaire) and Zambia; and the ALUR, who live in the northeast, between Congo (Zaire) and Uganda. Other groups include the LUBA of Kasai Region and Shaba (Katanga) Province in the south, KIVU in the east, HGBANDI, NBAKA, and MBANJA in the north, and LUNDA and YEKE in Shaba Province. These groups make up over 80 percent of the Congolese people; the rest are divided among a large number of smaller ethnic groups. About 80 percent of Congolese live in rural areas.

Language and religion: The official language of the country is French, but the most widely spoken languages are Lingala, Kikongo, and Swahili. Half of the Congolese practice their traditional religions; most of the rest are Christians.

History: Before it became independent of Belgium in June 1960, the country was known as the Belgian Congo. The BELGIANS left without preparing the people for self-rule. Terrible ethnic conflicts broke out almost immediately after independence.

The worst of these conflicts was when the Lunda and the Yeke, from the mineral-rich province of Katanga, tried to break away from the country. At first the Luba saw the struggle as a conflict between poor local people and rich foreigners. These foreigners were from among the Kasai Luba and the Chokwe peoples who had come to Katanga during the time of Belgian rule. Soon, however, the struggle became an ethnic one, and the local Luba joined the Kasai Luba and the Chokwe to oppose separation. The Katanga crisis ended in 1963. After that the country was ruled until recently by Mobutu Sese Seko, who changed its name to Zaire.

All groups living in Katanga continued to be unhappy that the government refused to return any of the money it took from their province or to invest in local development projects. In the 1970s there were two more crises, and the tension between the Lunda and Luba peoples are still there. In 1992 and 1993 many Luba fled Katanga (which Mobutu renamed Shaba) after violent attacks by the Lunda. Beginning in the early 1990s many people called for a democratic government. However, Mobutu harshly put down all who opposed him.

In 1997 a rebellion against the Mobutu government began in the eastern provinces of the country, near the boundary with Rwanda and Burundi, and spread to other parts of the country. The rebel force, led by Laurent Kabila, took control of the government. Kabila became the president and renamed the country the Democratic Republic of Congo.

CONGOLESE (Republic of Congo) The Congolese are the people that live in the Republic of Congo, in Africa.

Peoples and regions: There are almost 2.6 million people living in the country. The main **ethnic** groups include: the VILI, who live on the coast; the KONGO, who mainly live in the capital city of Brazzaville; and the TEKE, MBOCHI, and SANGHA, who make their home in the plains regions of the center and north of the country. Each of these ethnic groups is further divided into several smaller groups that share similar languages and cultures. About 50 percent of the Congolese practice their traditional religions, while the rest are mainly Christians. French is the official language of the Republic of Congo. However, Kikongo (the language of the Kongo people) and Teke are the most widely spoken.

Politics: The Congolese received freedom from the FRENCH in 1960. Since then differences among ethnic groups have made up a large part of the country's politics. There are divisions between the peoples of the north and south, and also between different groups in the north itself. The first two presidents of the Republic of Congo came from the south. However, after 1968 there were three presidents from the north who cared more about developing it. Even so, some of the northern people felt that the government was not helping them enough. Two events caused the president to take steps to give more people a say in the government in 1990: the Congolese people were unhappy with the way things were being run, and there was a serious economic emergency. A group was then formed to work on the the Republic of Congo's problems that included people from all over the country. It became a ruling organization.

COOK ISLANDERS The Cook Islanders are a group of the MAORI people. There are about 40,000 of them. Nineteen thousand of them live on 15 small islands in the southern part of the Pacific Ocean. Another 21,000 live in New

A Cook Islander dancer

Zealand. The Cook Islands are a self-ruled state associated with New Zealand.

Cook Islanders speak Maori, which is part of the Malayo-Polynesian language family. They practice different forms of Christianity. Over 90 percent of them are fishermen and farmers who grow coconuts, bananas, and citrus fruit. In the past few years tourism has become an important moneymaker for the islanders.

COPATAZA A group among the JIVARO in Ecuador.

COPTS see EGYPTIANS.

COR I A group among the JARAI in south-central Vietnam.

COR II A group among the SEDANG in southern Vietnam.

CORNISH (call themselves Kernow)   The Cornish are the people who live in the southwest part of England, in the county of Cornwall. Many of them have developed traditions of culture and language over the years that are different from the rest of the ENGLISH. In the past few years there has been a rebirth of the Cornish language, which was last used in the mideighteenth century. Many Cornish now speak their language in addition to English. They practice the Wesleyan form of Methodism, mixed with traces of **myths** and customs from their traditional religion. The Cornish economy is based on farming, tin and copper mining, fishing, and tourism.

CORSICANS   The Corsicans live on the island of Corsica. There are about 250,000 of them. Corsica has always been a poor island. Some of its people live in villages in the central part of the island; others are herders who wander with their herds. Many Corsicans have moved to France or Italy because of the island's poverty.

Religion and language: Most Corsicans are Catholic. They were ruled by the Genoese (from Italy) for many years. Since 1768 they have been controlled by France. French became the official language, but Corsicans still speak a **dialect** of Italian. They have also maintained many Italian customs and practices.

History and culture: The Corsicans are famous for certain cultural traits: they have large extended families and are known for the violent way they "solve" arguments. France stopped the activities of dangerous Corsican pirates; however, only the French Revolution fully brought the Corsicans into the French nation. This process was aided by the fact that the successful French emperor, Napoleon Bonaparte, was originally from Corsica. In the nineteenth century Corsicans tried to advance in French society by joining the French army or by moving to France. Many were involved when France took control of areas in other parts of the world. One hundred thousand Corsicans moved to Algeria, which was under French rule. Their return to Corsica in the 1960s helped make the island's economy more modern.

Economy and politics: Today Corsica's economic problems affect mainly the rural inland areas. Tourism earns money for the region. However, some Corsicans complain that tourism turns Corsica into an area that seems as if it is ruled by foreigners from within. The people who want Corsica to become independent have turned to violence to try to achieve their goals. In the 1980s the FRENCH officially pardoned the terrorists and gave some power to regional groups. Corsica was given even more self-rule in 1991.

COSSACKS (also called Zaporozhtsy)   see UKRAINIANS and KAZAKH.

COSTA RICANS   The Costa Ricans live in the Central American country of Costa Rica. It was under Spanish rule until 1821, when it won its independence. There are about 3.5 million Costa Ricans. About 95 percent of them come from different **ethnic** mixtures. There are several blends of *mestizos,* who are descendants of the Spanish settlers and Indians, with some African roots, too. Africans now make up two percent of the Costa Rican population, and CHINESE make up one percent.

Various Indian peoples lived in the area when the SPANIARDS conquered and settled it in the sixteenth century. Those Indians who survived the plagues and attacks that followed retreated to the highlands in the center of the country. In the nineteenth century coffee and then banana plantations were introduced into the country. These changed the nature of the society because there were not enough laborers to work the new plantations (too few Indians were left). Africans from Jamaica were brought in to work the fields. Their arrival had an influence on the ethnic and racial composition of the Costa Rican population.

People from other countries and cultures also have moved to Costa Rica. Between 1870 and 1920, 20-25 percent of population growth was from newcomers alone. But since 1920 there have been fewer immigrants.

Religion and culture: The official religion of Costa Rica is Roman Catholicism; 95 percent of Costa Ricans practice it. The Catholic church is still the most powerful institution in the country after the government, even though it has been weakened by the appearance of Christian preachers called evangelists. The Catholic church has played a large part in shaping Costa Rica's democratic society and has encouraged the government to create programs for the needy. The government looks after citizens who need help in education, health, and social services in a way that is similar to that of many European countries. The government also plays an important role in the country's economy. It controls banking, oil refining, and various large businesses like the gas and electric companies.

Native people: When the Europeans came to the region, many native groups were completely destroyed. However, there are still about 12 ethnic groups in Costa Rica, and two that originally come from native ethnic groups. After 500 years of control by outsiders, only six native languages are still in use. There are anywhere from 10,000 to 20,000 Indians living in Costa Rica today. Most of the official Indian **reservations** are near Costa Rica's border with Panama, in the Cordillera de Talamanca. Some reservations are further north, along the Pacific Ocean.

The Costa Rican natives are not a part of the main Costa Rican society and are isolated from each other geographically and culturally. The

A Costa Rican woman in a lodge kitchen

Indians farm their land for short periods of time and then leave it for a few years to renew itself before using it again. This method is useful in areas where there are few people.

The Indians have some serious environmental problems: they are losing more and more of their land, and others are taking advantage of the natural resources in their areas. There are laws to protect Indian cultures and land, but they are not really obeyed. Laws about drilling and mining directly affect the Indian lands. Even though they are supposed to protect Indian lands and people, the government can easily ignore them and get involved in mining. The Talamanca Indians made an agreement with the government to allow oil prospectry on their land. However, no one is sure that the agreement will really help protect the Indians.

The Indians make up less than one percent of the Costa Rican population. In the southern Caribbean region there are two main Indian groups: the CABECARE live in the areas of Moravia de Chirripo, Estrella, San Jose de Cabecar, Telire, and Pacuare; and the BIBRI live in the Talamanca valley and the nearby area of Cocles. There are also two groups in the northern Caribbean region: the GUATUSO and MALEKU mostly live in the areas of El Sol, Tonjibe, and Margarita on the Guatuso plains. The MISKITO group, also called Sambos Mosquitos, sometimes spend time in that area when they are moving around from place to place. The BORUCA, also called Brunka, live in the southern Pacific region, mainly in the areas of Boruca, Curre, and Maiz. The TERRABA, or Terbi, also live in the southern Pacific region in the Terraba area. A group of Cabecare live in Ujarraz, and some Bibri make their homes in Salitre and Cabagra. The GUAYMI live in Guaymi de Coto Brus, Abrojos-Montezuma, and Conte Burica along Costa Rica's border with Panama.

The ethnic groups that probably originally come from native Indian populations include: the CHOROTEGA groups in Matambu, Matambuguito, Guatil, Santa Barbara, and Hondores in the Guanacaste region; and a small group of HUETARES-PACACUAS in Quitirrise de Mora and Zapaton de Puriscal in the central region.

COTABATO MANOBO (also called Dulangon and Tudag) The Cotabato Manobo are an **ethnic** group that lives on the Philippine island of Mindanao. They make their homes in the southwestern mountains of Cotabato, mainly in the high, flat lands of the Kulaman Plateau. Their language is part of the Manobo family. The 16,000 Cotabato Manobo are farmers and also use wood from the forests nearby to make things to sell. They live in widely spread settlements of about 20 houses with straw roofs built on wooden pillars.

Religion: The Cotabato Manobo believe in a godlike figure named Namola. They think that after a person dies, his or her soul tries to reach Namola. In order to make that process easier, the Cotabato Manobo bury their dead only half-covered by earth. They also burn the dead person's house.

Native people: In 1971 a tiny group of about 70 people called the Tasaday was discovered. They are distantly related to the Cotabato Manobo. Experts used to believe that the Tasaday are what is left of a people who lived thousands of years ago during the Stone Age. Today many no longer believe that is true—even though the Tasaday are less developed than other peoples on the island. The Tasaday must be studied much more carefully before experts can properly place them among the peoples of the Philippines.

CÔTE D'IVOIRE, THE PEOPLE OF THE see IVOIREANS.

COURONIANS see LATVIANS.

COWICHAN The Cowichan are a Native North American group of several thousand that lives in

Canada along the southwestern coast of British Columbia and on Vancouver Island. They speak Halkomelem, a language of the Salishan family.

The Cowichan traditionally made a living by fishing and hunting sea mammals. Today many of them work in harvesting forest products and on fishing boats.

CREE The Cree are the largest Native North American group that lives in Canada. Most are found in the provinces of Quebec and Ontario (near St. James Bay) and in Manitoba, Saskatchewan, and Alberta. Over 100 more live in northern Montana. There are more than 130,000 Cree. Most of them were part of the Woodland Indians group. However, those living in Saskatchewan and in the southern part of Alberta were Plains Indians.

History and politics: The Big Bear Band in Saskatchewan was the last group of Plains Indians to move onto a **reservation** and the only group to violently fight the Canadians about moving. Many of today's Canadian Native North American leaders are Cree; Ovide Mercredi, who is the Chief of Assembly of First Nations of Canada, is a Cree.

After a long fight with the local and Canadian governments, the Cree living in Quebec decided to accept money in exchange for moving off their land. They had little choice because their land in northern Quebec was being flooded in order to create hydroelectric power. They used part of the money to buy an airline they call Air Cree. This made them the only Native Americans to have and run their own airline. In 1980 they fought the second stage of the electric power project (called the James Bay HydroElectric Project) and won.

Language: The various Cree bands share the Cree language, which belongs to the Algonkian family. There are many people who speak Cree

A Cree girl

Cree

today. There are also newspapers, books, and magazines available in Cree. It is even used in computer programs. (see also LUBICON)

CREEK (also called Abihki and Atasi) The Creek are a large Native North American tribe that used to live in Georgia and Alabama. They are also called the Creek Nation or Confederacy. They were moved to Oklahoma in the 1830s. Until 1906 they had their own Creek Nation government. Since there were so many Creek, and because they were very committed to their culture, they were able to maintain their language (Muskogee) and traditions. Today there are about 45,000 Creek. Most live on a **reservation** in Hughes and Tulsa Counties, Oklahoma, called the Creek Tribe Federal Trust Area.

CRIMEAN TATARS (call themselves Qyrym Tatarlyi, Qyrymly Tatar) The Crimean Tatars are an **ethnic** group of about 350,000 that lives today partly in the Crimean region of the Ukraine, partly in other areas of the former Soviet Union like Uzbekistan and also in neighboring countries.

Language: Their language is a member of the Kypchak group of the Turkic family. It has three **dialects**: the southern (coastal), central, and northern (plains). The southern dialect is very different from the other two; it is more like Turkish. The written language of Crimean Tatar is very similar to Osmanli Turkish. Isma'il Gasprinsky (or Gaspraly) changed parts of the written language and made it simpler. Its name was then changed to Turki, and it was used for the Turkic newspapers in the Russian Empire during the late nineteenth and early twentieth centuries. In the 1920s to 1930s the Crimean Tatar written language in the Soviet Union was changed to fit the central dialect. It used the Arabic alphabet until 1929, when that was replaced by the Roman alphabet (used for English). In 1938 it was changed again, this time to the Cyrillic alphabet (used for Russian).

History and religion: The Crimean Tatars are Sunni Muslims of the Hanafi school. They originally arrived in the Crimean area in the thirteenth century when a group called the Golden Horde TATARS came to the Crimean inner plains. The people who had been living there since at least the eleventh century, the Kypchak, were soon absorbed by the Tatars. Peoples who were not Turkic, like the GREEKS and the Goths, were also slowly absorbed. So were many Slavs who had been brought to Crimea as prisoners during the long wars between the Crimean Tatars and their neighbors. Crimea was taken over by the RUSSIANS from 1772 to 1783. During that time Crimean Christians were moved away from their homes to areas that the Russian government wanted to develop. This led many Christians (mostly Greeks from the coastal region) to convert to Islam. They also became more like the Tatars.

At the beginning of the nineteenth century the Russians pushed the Crimean Tatars to move out of Crimea and go to the Ottoman Empire. As a result, after 100 years of Russian rule the Crimean Tatar population in Crimea dropped from about 500,000 to 200,000. Most of those who had gone to Turkish regions of the Ottoman Empire were absorbed into the Turkish people. However, many of the descendants of the Crimean Tatars who had moved to non-Turkish parts of the Ottoman Empire still think of themselves today as Tatars (and not as Turks). There are 25,000 of them in Romania who are called Dobrudjan Tatars, and 10,000 in Bulgaria. In the 1980s there were 34,000 people living in Turkey who also thought of themselves as Tatars. They may originally have been Crimean Tatars or descendants of a few Tatars who came to Turkey at the beginning of the twentieth century because they believed that they were part of a greater Turkish group. Some may have also come to Turkey after the Russian Revolution in 1917. When the Soviet government created the Crimean Autonomous Republic in 1921, only about 25 percent of its population were Tatars. The rest were mainly Russians and UKRAINIANS.

In May 1944 the Crimean Tatars who were left in the Crimea were thrown out of their homes. The Soviets did this because they thought the Crimean Tatars had helped the **Nazis** when the GERMANS held control of the Crimea between 1941 and 1944. The Crimean Tatars were moved to areas in Central Asia, like Uzbekistan, to work as farmers. Half of them died on the way there. From the end of the 1950s the Soviets allowed them to put out their own newspapers and books in the Tashkent and Uzbekistan regions.

In 1967 the Soviets officially cleared the Crimean Tatars of the accusation that they had helped the Nazis during World War II but still did not allow them to go back to the Crimea. The Soviets had already moved many Slavs into areas where Crimean Tatars used to live. With the help of a group of educated Russians who were also protesting against the Soviet government, the

Crimean Tatars fought to return to the Crimea from the 1960s to the 1980s. These protests were among the strongest battles for independence in the Soviet Union. Many Crimean Tatars were put in jail. In November 1990 the government decided to let the Tatars return to the Crimea, but it put off carrying out this decision for a few years. However, when the Tatars started going back themselves, the Slav population in the Crimea was very hostile to them.

Culture: Crimean Tatars have lost much of their traditional lifestyle because they were forced out of their homes in 1944. The only aspect of their culture that they have not lost is their traditional food. They have been almost completely absorbed into the Russian culture. Almost all Crimean Tatars speak both Russian and Crimean Tatar. However, Russian is the first language of the younger people.

CRNO GORTSI see MONTENEGRINS.

CROATS (call themselves Hrvati) Most of the Croats live in Croatia, a country on the coast of the Adriatic Sea, in the northwestern part of what used to be Yugoslavia. There are about 5.5 million people living in Croatia, and 4.2 million of them are Croatian. About 800,000 lived in nearby Bosnia-Herzegovina until a civil war started there in 1991. Until that time they made up about a fifth of the population in Bosnia-Herzegovina. About 300,000 Croats lived in Serbia. The civil war has led to a great deal of chaos and caused many people to leave their homes, mainly for other European countries. About 200,000 Croats live outside of Europe, mainly in North America and Australia. They moved there after World War II.

Language: Croatian is a Slavic language in the Indo-European family. It is very similar to Serbian, and together the two languages make up one language called Serbo-Croat. However, the Croats use the Roman alphabet (used for English)

Top: Young Croats

Bottom: Croats celebrating in the central square of the old city of Dubrovnik

because they are Roman Catholic, while the SERBS, who are both neighbors and enemies of the Croats, use the Cyrillic alphabet (used for Russian).

Culture: Until the end of the nineteenth century it was traditional for three or four generations of one family to live together in one household. The extended family is called the *zadruga*. The father or grandfather was the head of the *zadruga*. The whole family shared work

Croats in one of the narrow streets of Dubrovnik, Croatia

and its results. However, the *zadruga* structure has fallen apart, especially in towns, because the Croatian culture has changed over the last 200 years.

History: Slavic tribes moved to the Panonian plains in the south-central part of Europe in the first centuries of this era. After crossing the Carpathian Mountains, the Slavic ancestors of the Croats settled down mainly in the plains areas near the Drava and Sava rivers. They also settled

in the Dalmatian Mountain area near the Adriatic Sea. In the ninth century they were converted to Christianity by Roman Catholic **missionaries**. Their neighbors, the Serbs, became Greek Orthodox Christians.

In 880 Branislav became the first independent duke, or ruler, of Croatia. Kresimir II, also called Kresimir the Great, ruled from 1000 to 1035. He conquered a large part of the Dalmatian area, including some Italian ports on the Adriatic Sea.

A decorated street in Dubrovnik, Croatia

By that time the Croats had built up a strong navy. They used their skills and ships at first to act as pirates and later for trade. They competed with Venice, which had the strongest navy on the Adriatic Sea. By the end of the eleventh century Croatia was ruled by King Zvonimir, and he made it one of the strongest countries in the Balkans area.

Croatia became part of the kingdom of Hungary by its own choice in 1102. It maintained some self-rule under its own *ban,* or ruler. In the sixteenth century the Ottoman Empire threatened to invade Croatia and Hungary. At that time Croatia (which was part of Hungary) became part of the Habsburg Empire. But by the early seventeenth century most of Croatia had been taken over by the Ottoman Empire. Only a small area in the western part of Croatia stayed under Austrian and Hungarian rule. However, the peace treaty of Carlowitz (1699) gave all of Croatia back to the Habsburgs. Under the Habsburgs the Croatians maintained a certain amount of self-rule until 1840. They were able to use the Croatian language for official purposes. At one point the empire tried to make Hungarian the official language. This led the Croatians to want an independent country of their own, and soon a movement was started to unite all southern Slavs. These desires caused the Slavs to rebel against the empire in 1848, but the rebellion was quickly put down. In the late nineteenth century they continued to fight for self-rule and even a state for the southern Slavs.

In 1917 a group of Croatian leaders forced to live in London, in **exile** from their homeland, signed an agreement with the Serbian government. It was called the Corfu Declaration. The agreement stated that the southern Slavs of Austria-Hungary would be united with Serbia and Montenegro, which were independent countries. This led to the creation in 1918 of the kingdom of Yugoslavia ("Yugo" means "southern"). However, the Croats were soon disappointed with the small role they were given in their new kingdom. They wanted more independence. A group called the Croatian Peasant Party, led by Stjepan Radic, argued that the Serbs should not have so much power in the kingdom. Radic was killed by his enemies in 1928, which led to more anger and fighting between the Croats and the Serbs.

During World War II a Croat group called the *Ustase* used the excuse that the Germans had

conquered Yugoslavia in April 1941 to declare an independent Croatian country. Both the Germans and the *Ustase,* led by Ante Pavelic, believed in having total control over the people, and they fought together on the same side to make as big a state as possible. However it threw out and murdered members of different **ethnic** groups, including Serbs, JEWS, and GYPSIES. The *Ustase* fought against two groups that wanted freedom for Yugoslavia: the Yugoslavian government-in-exile in London and the Communist government, led by a Croat named Tito.

After the war in 1946 Croatia became one of Yugoslavia's six separate but united republics. Tito became leader of all of Yugoslavia. He did not give independence to any of the ethnic groups under his control and forbade any independence movements. However, when Tito died in 1980, the Serbs and Croats began fighting again. In the summer of 1991 Croatia declared itself an independent country and no longer part of Yugoslavia. The Serbs objected to this and started a war against Croatia. This war led the important countries of the world to accept Croatia as a separate state.

Later, in 1992, the Croats of nearby Bosnia-Herzegovina became involved in a civil war involving them, the Serbs, and BOSNIAN MUSLIMS. The Croats there fought against the Bosnian Muslims from time to time. Eventually the Croats and the Bosnian Muslims joined forces in a Croat-Bosnian Federation against the Bosnian Serbs. (see also BOSNIAN MUSLIMS, SERBS, SLOVENES)

CROW (also called Absaroka) The Crow are a Native North American group. Most Crow live in Montana. They used to live in the Yellowstone area and in parts of the Dakotas. Many were killed during the nineteenth century by the SIOUX Indians. Today there are about 6,500 Crow.

The Crow were one of the first Native North American groups to practice the Sun Dance religion. It is still part of their religious tradition. Every August they host a meeting, called a powwow, which is the largest gathering today of Plains Indians in the United States and Canada. The Crow **reservation** is now partly flooded by the waters of the Yellowtail Dam.

CUA (also called Khua) An **ethnic** group of about 10,000 that lives in the hilly area of the central part of Vietnam. The Cua speak a Mon-Khmer language.

CUBANS The Cubans live in Cuba, the largest of the Caribbean Islands. It is found where the Atlantic Ocean, the Gulf of Mexico, and the Caribbean Sea meet. There are 11 million Cubans living on the island, and another 1.5 million living in other places, mainly in the United States.

Peoples and history: The Cubans come from several different groups that mixed together after the Europeans arrived in the area. These include: the Ciboneyes and Taino Indians who were living on the island when it was discovered by Europeans; the SPANIARDS; African slaves; and a small group of CHINESE newcomers who arrived in Cuba in the middle of the 1800s.

After the Spaniards came to Cuba and took control, most of the Indian population died out. Many died of diseases that they were not used to that the Spaniards brought. The Spaniards also murdered many of them and worked others to death. Those Indians who survived and were given freedom generally adopted Spanish culture. Many Indian women married Spaniards because the Spanish did not bring along enough women of their own.

At first the white population of Cuba was made up only of the Spanish conquerors, called in Spanish *conquistadores.* Later, many other Spaniards came to Cuba, mainly from the regions of Andalusia, the Canary Islands, and Asturias in Spain. Spaniards went back and forth to Cuba frequently during that period.

In the early sixteenth century the first black slaves from Africa came to Cuba. Havana, the capital of Cuba, became an important slave market. By the mid-1800s there were more blacks there than whites. Some black slaves came from West Africa, mainly from Senegal and the Republic of Congo. The largest and most important group of African slaves in Cuba were the YORUBA, who came from the southwestern part of Nigeria. The influence of the Yoruba on Cuban culture is still felt today, through food, music, and other cultural aspects.

The Spaniards saw that the African population in Cuba was growing, so they tried to get more whites to come to Cuba. However, they were not very successful. Some people in the government then suggested that they bring in Chinese workers because the Chinese were strong and could take the place of the black slaves. The Chinese came to Cuba and worked in the sugar cane fields to pay off travel money that the Cubans had given them. This type of labor was similar to the older slave trade; companies took advantage of the new workers. The Chinese were good and intelligent workers who often made enough money to start their own businesses. Most of the Chinese who came to Cuba were men, so many of them married women from other **ethnic** groups, especially white *criollo* women (Spaniards born in the New World).

Instead of concentrating on the differences between racial groups, the Cubans have paid more attention to the political differences between those born in Cuba and Spaniards or other foreigners. However, there has also been prejudice against certain races in Cuban society. Before 1959 blacks were not allowed to go to the better beaches, hotels, and the places of entertainment where AMERICANS and upper-class Cubans spent time. The upper and middle classes were mostly white, while blacks and mulattoes (people with both black and white parents) were among the poorest in the society. Nonwhites who

Top: Cuban farmers
Bottom: Cuban children at the entrance to their home

A Cuban working in a cigar factory

had some white features had an easier time improving their social status. Partly because of this, there were many mulatto Cubans who were part of the middle or upper middle social classes. They were mostly skilled workers.

Language: The national language of Cuba is Spanish. Its accent and expressions are similar to the Spanish of Andalusia. There is also a lot of African influence on Cuban Spanish, and some Taino Indian words have entered the language. In addition, because the United States is so close to Cuba, many English words have found their way into Cuban Spanish.

Religion: About 85 percent of Cubans are said to be Catholics. This is probably true in name only; the Catholic Church says that only about 10 percent really practice the religion. Catholicism in Cuba never had the number of followers that it had in other Latin America countries. Mainly only upper-class Cubans living in the cities are Catholics. However, a large part of Cuban culture *is* based on Catholic beliefs and ceremonies. Poorer Cubans mixed Catholicism with Afro-Cuban religions. One religion, called Santeria, includes practices from its participants' traditional ethnic backgrounds and sometimes adds Catholic customs. It has given African names to Catholic saints.

People began to practice Protestantism in Cuba during the late 1800s. They were influenced by the Protestant movements in the United States. The United States conquered Cuba in 1898–1902, and the number of Protestants grew. The Southern Baptist, Methodist, Presbyterian, and Episcopalian churches had many Cuban followers by the 1950s. This is partly because the poorer Cubans felt comfortable with Protestantism, and the Protestant leaders were more accepting of the goals of the Socialist revolution in Cuba than the Catholics.

Politics and Nationalism: In 1959 there was a Communist revolution in Cuba led by Fidel Castro that had very radical goals. They included removing as much economic inequality and unfairness in Cuban society as possible. After about a year the poor were very happy with this goal. However, most of the upper and middle class rejected it because it meant they would have to share their wealth with the poor. This new economic plan also led to a ban by the United States (which opposes Communism) against Cuba, which included not letting anyone trade with Cuba. Many Cubans (mostly from the white upper and middle class) began to leave their country starting in the 1960s. Most of these people entered the United States and were viewed as people fleeing from an undesirable Cuban government. However, the Cubans who have left Cuba in the past few years come from all parts of the society, not just the upper class.

The Cuban people have very strong feelings about their homeland. This goes back to the time when the *criollos* fought to be different from the Spaniards in all areas, including art, science, and politics. These feelings of *Cubania,* meaning "Cuban-ness," lasted a long time because Cuba was the last of the Spanish-controlled areas in the Americas to get its freedom. Cuba gained independence from Spain in 1898 and was taken over for a short time (until 1902) by the United States. After finally getting its freedom, it still had very strong feelings about independence and protested against the United States continually interfering in its economy and politics.

The largest number of Cubans outside Cuba is in Miami, Florida. Many of the Cubans who live there show their desire for Cuban freedom by protesting strongly and radically against Castro and his Communist government. Even more middle-of-the-road groups both in Miami and in Cuba often express their desire for full independence. However, they prefer to use talking and listening, instead of fighting, to solve Cuba's many problems.

CUMANANGOTO A Native South American group that lives in Venezuela.

CUNA The Cuna are a South American Indian people who live in Panama. The Cuna used to have a complicated religion and class system. Today they are farmers living in small villages. They raise pigs and chickens to trade. Because they have adopted much of the culture of the people around them, the Cuna wear Western clothing instead of their traditional outfits. Their religion has traditional and magical aspects to it.

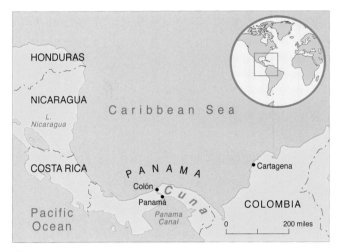

Cuna

CURAÇAOANS The island of Curaçao is found in the Caribbean Sea off the northern coast of Venezuela. It is part of the Netherlands Antilles Islands, which is a self-governing part of the Netherlands. There are about 150,000 people in Curaçao. Most of them are descendants of Africans because Curaçao was the center of the Caribbean slave trade during the years when Europeans controlled the area. However, there are also more than 40 other groups living in Curaçao. The official language is Dutch, but English and a language common to the whole area, called Papiamento, are also spoken. Papiamento is a mixture of Dutch and English, along with French, Spanish, Portuguese, Arawak, and African words.

una women sit together sewing their famous molakana

CUNA CLOTHES

n the Atlantic Coast of Panama ves a group of people called the UNA. Many centuries ago the Cuna ved only in the middle of Panama id northern Colombia, but nearly 00 years ago they began moving oward the eastern part of Panama. he Cuna are known for many iings, but they are best known for ieir traditional beautiful women's louses called *molakana* (singular *ola*).

The word mola means "material" r "dress." It is a short-sleeved oman's blouse that is decorated in ont and back with many different iapes and designs, each of which as a special meaning. These esigns are made by sewing various ieces of material on top of one

another. Before beginning, the designs are drawn in chalk onto the material, and then cutting and sewing can begin. A beginner usually starts with smaller pieces of material, which have her designs sewn on; but an expert craftswoman can work on several blouses at the same time. The designs found on molakana vary from traditional pictures of animals or plants to modern appliances, cars, or even helicopters. They are often hard for non-Cuna to understand, but they have special meaning for Cuna women. There are no rules about what designs can go on a mola, except that the designs have to be beautiful and festive.

Cuna women began making molakana at the end of the nineteenth century. Before that they

lived in the rainforests of Central America, and the hot, humid, weather forced them to dress extremely lightly. Women wore only a plain grass skirt, and men wore a loincloth. However, when the Cuna began to settle near the Atlantic Ocean, they began to have many contacts with European travelers and businessmen. The cooler weather forced them to begin wearing more clothes, and their clothing styles were influenced by the Europeans. After a while, the men stopped wearing their traditional golden nose rings and began to wear shirts, pants, and hats (and even suits and ties on festive occasions). Today, the traditional outfit worn by Cuna women consists of a skirt, cloth head covering, and jewelry; but these are usually made

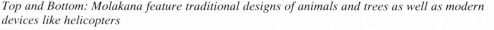

Top and Bottom: Molakana feature traditional designs of animals and trees as well as modern devices like helicopters

The stages in making a mola. The mola is made of several layers of material sewn on top of each other. From these layers a Cuna woman cuts and sews the design. The detail is done by putting on layers of brightly colored material, which are gradually cut out and sewn in. An experienced Cuna woman can make several molakana at one time

in other places and purchased by the Cuna people. It is only the mola that is made by the Cuna themselves.

In addition to the beauty of the mola there is a great deal of cultural meaning to these garments. Young girls are taught by their mothers the art of sewing; and when a girl finishes her first mola, there is a great celebration. New molakana are generally reserved for official ceremonies, and they are treated with a great deal of respect. Until the 1970s, outsiders were only allowed to buy used molakana, but today, tourists and collectors are can now buy new ones. Molakana are also sold to art museums and department stores in the United States, Europe and Japan.

Among the Cuna, women are the main keepers of the home. When they have done their cooking and cleaning chores, they are expected to use their free time to make molakana. Even during formal public ceremonies that can last many hours, Cuna women must keep busy making the molakana that have made them famous.

Curaçao's economy is based on the island's oil refineries. The oil business has also encouraged other businesses to develop, such as shipbuilding, trade, and air traffic.

CUSULIMA   A group among the JÍVARO in Ecuador.

CUYO   A Native South American group that lives in Argentina.

CWABO   see CHUABO.

CYMRU   see WELSH.

CYPRIOTS   The Cypriots are the people that live on the island of Cyprus in the eastern part of the Mediterranean Sea. They are divided into two **ethnic** groups: the Greek Cypriots and the

Turkish Cypriots. Each celebrates its own national and religious holidays and feels part of its "motherland" (Greece or Turkey). There are about 750,000 Cypriots. About 80 percent of them are GREEKS who speak Greek and are Greek Orthodox Christians; 18 percent are Turkish-speaking Sunni Muslim TURKS. There are also a few thousand ARMENIANS and Maronite Christians in Cyprus. Turks and Greeks live all over the island. One-sixth of the country's villages were mixed between the two groups until 1974. At that time Cyprus was invaded by Turkey, which separated the two groups.

History: By 1000 B.C. or even earlier the ancient Greeks had conquered Cyprus. After them other groups invaded, including the Phoenicians, Ptolemies, and Romans. The people of Cyprus were converted to Christianity in the first century and Cyprus had a large degree of

Cypriots

A Greek Cypriot on his donkey

self-rule in the Byzantine Empire. Cyprus was the ruled first by French Latins and later by Venetian Latins from the twelfth century until 1571. At that point the Ottoman Turks took over. New Muslim settlers began arriving in Cyprus, especially in the northeast corner, instead of the Westerners who had been there before. The Muslims, who eventually saw themselves as Turkish Cypriots, treated the Greek Orthodox Cypriots better than the Latins had.

In the eighteenth century a Greek Orthodox religious leader called the *ethnarch* became responsible for collecting taxes from the Greeks. This practice led to the importance of the church in Cyprus's economy and politics until today. Greeks in Greece in the nineteenth century began to feel that they wanted all Greeks to have their own independent state, and this caused the Greek Cypriots to feel the same. Church leaders led the fight for *enosis,* which means joining Cyprus with Greece. However, throughout most of the time that the Ottoman Turks were in control of Cyprus, the Greek and Turkish Cypriots lived together peacefully (even though they did not have much social contact). In 1878 the BRITISH took control of Cyprus, while the Ottomans still officially ruled the area. Britain set up a navy base there to use against Russia. Turkey gave up its power over Cyprus in 1923, and Britain was completely in charge. Thousands of Turkish Cypriots left Cyprus for Turkey. That is why the population of Cyprus today is mostly Greek Cypriot. Greek Cypriots were happy that the British came because they thought the British would help them with *enosis* (uniting with Greece). The Turkish Cypriots, however, hoped that the British would stop *enosis.* They feared that if Cyprus joined Greece, then Turkish Cypriots would be outnumbered and in

A Greek Cypriot shepherd

danger. From the 1930s many Cypriots fought the British and their power over Cyprus. Greek Cypriots looked at Crete, another Greek island that had finally been united with Greece after 100 years of fighting, as a good example of what they could do. On the other hand, Turkish Cypriots saw Crete as an example of Muslims being thrown out of their homes. The Greek Cypriots wanted freedom to move around and settle freely all over Cyprus; the Turkish Cypriots thought that would make the fact that they were outnumbered even worse. They called for separation between the ethnic groups and finally for dividing Cyprus. In the 1950s the Greek Cypriots became even more radical. They elected Michael Mouskos, who was very strongly for *enosis,* as Archbishop Makarios III. Another group fighting for *enosis* was the military group EOKA, led by Giorgios Grivas. Because of the stubbornness of these groups, they could agree on nothing except *enosis.*

In 1960 the British decided to give Cyprus some self-rule. However, by that time so many Greek and Turkish Cypriots had been killed that neither of the two groups wanted to live with the other. The two groups accepted a joint body of laws; however, they could not agree on a shared police force. Violence broke out in 1963. The Greek Cypriots attacked the Turkish Cypriots, who moved into guarded villages. But their areas were blockaded by Greek Cypriots, and they had to depend on Turkey for economic help. The island was in fact split between them.

In 1974 the Greek Army, which wanted to attach Cyprus to Greece, encouraged the Greek Cypriots to overthrow Makarios. This led Turkey to invade Cyprus. The Greek and Turkish Cypriots attacked each other, and each group removed the other from their homes. What followed was an official separation, or partition. Sixty-two percent of the area of Cyprus is under the control of the Greek Cypriots, while 38 percent of the land is held by Turkish Cypriots. In 1983 the Turks declared themselves an

independent country. At that time tens of thousands of Turkish Cypriots fled to north Cyprus, and 200,000 Greek Cypriots moved to the south, where the Greek Cypriots were in power. This brought an entirely new challenge to Cyprus. In the past the Cypriots had to decide how the two ethnic groups should share power. Now they had to work out a way to build a connection between two ethnic groups living in two divided areas. Peace-keepers from the United Nations stay on and patrol an area between the groups' separate territories.

Since 1976 the United Nations has supported peace talks between the two groups. The Greek Cypriots want a strong union of the groups, but the Turkish Cypriots are not as interested. Talks continued throughout the 1980s, but little came of them. As time passes, the division between the two ethnic groups in Cyprus gets deeper.

Economy: The Greek area of Cyprus is quite wealthy; it has a higher standard of living than the mainland of Greece. After taking in all the fleeing Greek Cypriots, the area began to grow in wealth in the 1980s. Its economy depends heavily on the major tourism industry that developed there in the last few years. The Turkish Cypriot area, however, has hardly any tourism. It has a poor economy and is the victim of an international ban. Salaries in the Turkish part of Cyprus are four times lower than those in the Greek part. Even so, thousands of Turks from mainland Turkey have moved to Cyprus and taken over houses where Greeks used to live. This has raised the Turkish Cypriot population to 153,000.

CZECHS (call themselves Cehi) The Czechs are a group of people who live mostly in the Czech Republic. The Czech Republic is home to 10 million Czechs. Some Czechs live in nearby Poland, Slovakia, and Austria. There are also groups of Czechs in North America and Eastern and Western Europe. There are 11.3 million Czechs altogether.

A Czech coachman in the central square of ancient Prague

Language: The Czech language is part of the Western Slavic group. It is very similar to Slovak, and speakers of the two languages can understand one another. Czech has had a written form since the fifteenth century and uses the Roman alphabet (used for English). Until the nineteenth century Czech was also the written language of the Slovaks.

Culture: Although the Czechs and Slovaks have similar origins, languages, and religious beliefs (both groups are mostly Catholic), they have different cultures. Czech culture was heavily influenced by the GERMANS, while the Slovak culture had Hungarian influences. The Czechs are one of the most modern Slavic peoples. They also have the most advanced education system, culture, and economy, including many modern factories and businesses.

History: The Czechs originally came from Slavic tribes that moved into the areas of Bohemia and Moravia in the fifth and sixth centuries. Their name was taken from a Bohemian tribe that named itself for one of their heroes. By the ninth century a number of tribes divided into separate states. The strongest state, Great Moravia, was formed in the Morava River valley. This area was a central trade route between the Baltic and Adriatic seas. Great Moravia spread out all over Bohemia and Moravia, part of Slovakia, the southern part of what is today Poland, and the western part of Hungary. At that time the country became Christian. For a long time it could not decide whether to accept the religious leadership of Rome or Constantinople but finally chose the Catholicism of Rome. It first used Slavonic to conduct its religious services, and then switched to Latin.

At the beginning of the tenth century the HUNGARIANS attacked Great Moravia, and it fell. The Premysl dynasty then ruled the Czechs from their castle in Praha (Prague). They were able to bring Bohemia and later Moravia under their control. The Premysl rulers, who held power from 895 to 1306, brought Bohemia into the Holy Roman Empire. The empire awarded them the title "King of Bohemia." The Premysls brought in many Germans to settle the area and made Prague into one of the greatest centers of culture and learning of the time.

When the Premysl rulers died out, the kingdom of Bohemia was ruled by the House of Luxembourg (1310–1437). Karl, the king of Bohemia, was also made emperor of the Holy Roman Empire in 1355 as Karl or Charles IV. Prague became his capital, and he made it a beautiful city with very attractive buildings. He also created the University of Prague. However, after Karl died, the country became involved in the religious disputes in the Catholic church called the Reformation. In 1405 a man named Jan Hus was killed after he tried to get the church to make some changes. After he died, the country

Czech workers rolling down a keg of beer from a truck

was divided into his followers, called Hussites, and Catholics.

In the sixteenth century Ferdinand I of Habsburg was elected leader. This began almost 400 years of rule by the Habsburg family (until 1918). During the Thirty Years' War the Habsburgs and Catholicism became very important and accepted in Bohemia and Moravia. Later the country's culture became quite similar to that of Germany.

In the early 1800s the Czech people began to want freedom. At first the Czechs joined with Germans who were also looking for independence. But during the revolutions of 1848 a German group in Frankfurt declared Bohemia and Moravia part of Germany. This led the Czechs to pull away from the Germans. During the nineteenth century the Czechs changed their focus from wanting partial self-rule within the Habsburg Empire to a desire for total freedom. They also made connections with other Slavic groups in the empire, especially with the Slovaks. This union led to the creation of the country of Czechoslovakia in 1918.

There were twice as many Czechs as Slovaks in the new country, and the Czechs were also more wealthy. This led the Czechs to be the more important group in Czechoslovakia. The Slovaks began to feel upset about their lower position. At the same time, there were about 2.5 million Germans and many Hungarians under the control of the democratic government of Czechoslovakia, which allowed different **ethnic** groups the freedom to think and act as they wanted. The **Nazis**, who ruled Germany at the time, used this as an excuse to cut up Czechoslovakia and end its democracy after the Munich Conference in 1938.

Czechoslovakia was put back together again after World War II, and the Germans were thrown out. In 1948 a Communist government took control in Prague, and Czechoslovakia came under strong Soviet influence. In 1968 some Czechs tried to change the Communist government and make it more open and fair. This was called the "Prague Spring." It did not last very long because the Soviet Army arrived and ended the protest. After that, until the Communist government fell in 1990, Czechoslovakia was one of the strictest Communist countries in Eastern Europe. In 1969 it was divided into two republics under the control of one government. After the Communists fell, both the Czech and Slovak desire for independent countries grew stronger. In January 1993 the two groups decided to become separate independent states, the Czech Republic and Slovakia, each with its own government. (see also SLOVAKS)

D

DABA An **ethnic** group among the KIRDI in Chad.

DADOG see BARABAIG.

DAFI An **ethnic** group that lives in northwest Burkina Faso. They speak the Marka language, which belongs to the Mande family, and are Muslims.

DAFLA (call themselves Nishang, Nisi) The Dafla are an **ethnic** group of about 250,000 people. They live in the Subansiri area of Arunachal Pradesh, India. Their language is part of the Tibeto-Burman family.

   The Dafla are a warlike people. They build houses that are sometimes 2,000 feet long. The walls are made of woven mats, and the floors of flattened bamboo. Dafla men marry more than one wife. Sometimes more than 10 families live in one house, and each wife has her own separate corner.

   The Dafla grow rice—their main food—and millet. When their fields get worn out, they move to other ones. They also eat fish, meat from different animals, root vegetables, and leafy vegetables.

DAGABA (also callet Dagari, Dagati) The Dagaba are a people numbering 800,000. About 500,000 live in northeast Ghana and 300,000 in southwest Burkina Faso. They speak Dagaari, a language that is part of the Niger-Congo family. Some are Muslim or Christian, and many maintain aspects of their traditional religion.

DAGANA A group among the HASSAUNA in Chad.

DAGARI see DAGABA.

DAGATI see DAGABA.

DAGBAMBA see DAGOMBA.

DAGBON see DAGOMBA.

DAGOMBA (also called Dagbon; call themselves Dagbamba) The Dagomba are an **ethnic** group of 550,000 that lives in northeastern Ghana. They speak the Dagbane language, which is part of the Niger-Congo family. Most are Muslims, but some keep their traditional religion or practice Christianity. In their society men are the leaders, and inheritance passes from father to son.

   Before Europeans ruled the area, the Dagomba lived in the kingdom of MOLE-DAGBANI. It was conquered by the GERMANS in the late nineteenth century. Part of the kingdom became German Togoland, and part became the British Gold Coast (now called Ghana). When the Germans lost World War I, all of Dagomba territory came under British rule.

DAHAYAT The Dahayat are a people who live mainly in the Indian state of Madhya Pradesh. There are about 450,000 of them. They are closely related to the KOL people, and they practice the Hindu religion. During the time that India was ruled by princes, the Dahayat had important jobs in government and in palace ceremonies.

DAI The Dai live mostly in Yunnan Province of southwest China. They also can be found in Thailand (where they are called TAI), Burma, Laos, and Vietnam. There are about 840,000 Dai. They are closely related to the THAIS in Thailand.

Language and religion: They speak a Tai language whose written form comes from the ancient Indian.

Most Dai are Buddhists. Most young men spend time as monks, leading a strict religious life. Buddhist temples, the monasteries where monks live, are the social and religious centers in many villages. Other traditional religious beliefs are also common.

History and culture: The Dai first appeared as a culture about 3,000 years ago in the area south of the Yangtze River in present-day south-central China. They were forced to move south by the HAN CHINESE, who were taking over new territory as they spread to the south of China.

The Dai live in wooden houses, which they build off the ground on wooden pillars. They farm mainly with plows. Historical records from as early as the ninth century describe how the Dai used elephants and cattle to pull their plows. In modern times they have learned ways of bringing streams of water to their fields, which allows them to grow rice.

The Dai have maintained their traditional culture in most ways, including their traditional clothing, religion, and language. (see also HANI, SHAN)

DAIRI see PAKPAK.

DAJU The Daju live in northern Sudan in the Nuba Mountains of Darfur Province. Some also live in hard-to-reach areas on the border with Chad. There are about 28,000 Daju.

They speak Daju, a language of the Eastern Sudanic family. Some also speak Arabic.

The Daju are farmers and cattle-raisers. Most practice the Muslim religion. Even so, they have maintained many of their traditional religious beliefs and practices.

DAKARKARI (call themselves Lela) A group among the HAUSA-FULANI people in Nigeria. They number about 100,000. They speak Lela, a Niger-Congo language. They mostly maintain their traditional religion, but some are Muslims. They are grain farmers.

DAKOTA see SIOUX.

DAKPA A group among the BANDA people in the Central African Republic.

DALABON An Australian Aboriginal group that lives in the Northern Territory of Australia. (see also AUSTRALIAN ABORIGINES)

DAMARA The Damara are a group that speaks the Nama language. The 120,000 Damara live in western Namibia. They work mainly in farming. (see also NAMIBIANS)

DAMBONO An **ethnic** group that lives in Gabon. They are related to the KOTA people.

DAMELI The Dameli are an **ethnic** group of 6,000 that lives in the Chitral region of northern Pakistan, east of the Kunar River. They came originally from Afghanistan.

Their traditional language contains some aspects of Nuristani and some aspects of Dardic. In fact, the Dameli language may be a link between those two groups. The language has no written form; the Dameli use Urdu for writing and education.

The Dameli are Isma'ili Muslims. They are farmers who live in permanent settlements but also keep herds in the mountain valleys.

DAMI see DIME.

DAMPELASA An **ethnic** group that lives on Kalimantan (also called Borneo), an island in Indonesia. (see also DAYAK)

DAN (also called Gio) The Dan are an **ethnic** group that lives in Nimba County, Liberia, where they number about 200,000. Another 800,000 Dan also live in the far western part of the Ivory Coast (near the towns of Man and Danané). About 75,000 are found in nearby Guinea. The YACOUBA are a subgroup of the Dan. They speak the Dan language, which is part of the Mande family.

They mainly practice their traditional religions, even though there have been attempts to convert them to Islam. In the early twentieth century the Dan came under FRENCH rule when France took over the Ivory Coast despite their strong opposition.

In Liberia (where they are known as Gio) the Dan have been part of that country's ongoing civil war. They joined with the MANO and the KISSI people to fight against the KRAHN. Many Dan have fled to the Ivory Coast and Guinea to get away from the fighting.

The Dan are farmers who grow rice and manioc for food, and coffee and cocoa to sell to other countries. (see also IVOIREANS)

DANAKIL An insulting name that neighbors call the AFAR people.

DANES The Danes are the people of Denmark. There are about 5.3 million of them, and over 90 percent are Lutheran Protestants. About one-quarter of all Danes live in the capital city, Copenhagen. The Danish language is part of the Scandinavian branch of the Germanic family.

History: Today's Danes originally came from the tribe of Danes who came to the area from Sweden in the sixth century. They mixed with the Jutes and FRISIANS, peoples who had been living there. In the ninth century all Danish-speaking groups became a united people in Denmark. At that point southern Sweden was also part of Danish territory.

Danish seamen joined with the Vikings who attacked and robbed settlements along the coasts of France and Spain and who conquered Normandy and part of England. Danish sailors also did a great deal of damage to the Carolingian Empire and destroyed Celtic kingdoms in the British Isles. Because of this Danish influence the Danish language was spoken in parts of England until the twelfth century. For many years the

A Danish guard in front of the Royal Palace in Copenhagen

A Dane burning wood for charcoal

Danes practiced Germanic religions that involved idol worship. However, by the tenth and eleventh centuries most Danes had become Christians. When the Danes adopted Lutheran Protestantism from the Germans, they also took on aspects of German culture.

In the late Middle Ages the Danes controlled Norway and Sweden as well as Pomerania, Courland, and Estland on the Baltic Sea coast. Later the half-German Schleswig-Holstein areas also became part of Denmark. In 1523 Denmark lost control of Sweden, and for 300 years those two countries remained enemies. In the mid-seventeenth century Denmark fought and lost a series of terrible wars against Sweden. After that Denmark was no longer a great power. Even after it united with Norway in 1720, Denmark did not regain its former power.

In 1815 the Danes lost Norway to Sweden. Also during that century the people in Schleswig-Holstein began to identify more and more with their German nationality. This was especially true in Holstein, which wanted to become independent from Denmark (in Schleswig, by contrast, Danish feelings were stronger). In 1864 Denmark lost the whole of the Schleswig-Holstein area when Prussia took it over. During the late nineteenth century Danes who were now living in German territory suffered because they were not allowed to fully express their culture. Tens of thousands moved back to Denmark or overseas.

After World War I the parts of northern Schleswig that had many Danes living in them voted to become part of Denmark. Southern Schleswig joined Germany. Most of the Danish people in Southern Schleswig have adopted German language and culture.

DANGLA A group among the NUBIAN of Sudan.

Danwar

DAGME see ADANGBE.

DANI The Dani are an **ethnic** group that lives on the Indonesian part of the island of New Guinea. They make their home in the mountains near the Balim River in the eastern Irian Jaya area. There are over 250,000 of them.

They speak a number of local New Guinean languages that are related to one another. They grow sweet potatoes and raise pigs. The traditional religion of the Dani involved beliefs about spirits of their dead, and most of their rituals were related to war. Today, however, most Dani are Christians.

DANJO A group among the SEMANG people in Malaysia.

DANOA (also called Haddad) The Danoa are an **ethnic** group of about 100,000 people who are divided into 40 **clans** that are scattered throughout northern Chad. Thirty percent of them live in the Kanem region. The Danoa have no language of their own; they speak the languages of the people among whom they live. However,

they usually marry only members of their own group.

DANWAR The Danwar are an **ethnic** group that lives south of Kathmandu, the capital of Nepal. They practice the Hindu religion but also worship other gods. They do not marry members of other **castes**. They speak Danwar, an Indo-Aryan language, but very few can read and write.

The Danwar farm, fish, breed cattle, and sell goats and buffalo.

DARASA (also called Gedicho) The Darasa are a people numbering about 500,000 who live east of Lake Abaya in northern Sidamo Province, Ethiopia. Their language is part of the eastern Cushitic group. Some are Sunni Muslims, others are Ethiopian Orthodox Christians, but most still maintain their traditional beliefs.

The Darasa are farmers. They grow grains and the bananalike ensete plant for food. They also grow coffee to sell.

Their society used to be divided into **clans** with councils of elders who governed and made decisions. People are given honor and power according to their age and their generation in a way that is similar to the OROMO people. (see ETHIOPIANS, OROMO)

Darasa

Dargin

DARD see KOHISTANI.

DARGHIN see DARGIN.

DARGIN (also called Darghin; call themselves Dargwa) The Dargin are an **ethnic** group that lives in the mountains of central Daghestan in the Russian Federation. They are found between the Caspian Sea and the valley where the Qaziqumukh Koisu River flows. There are 370,000 Dargin.

Religion: Most Dargin are Sunni Muslims of the Shafi'i school; however, two villages are Shi'ite Muslim. The Dargin became Muslims gradually between the eleventh and sixteenth centuries.

Language: The Dargin language is part of the central group of the Daghestani branch of the North Caucasian family. It has had a written form since the nineteenth century. Until 1928 the Dargin had used the Arabic alphabet; in 1928 a new alphabet was created using Roman letters (used for English); this was changed in 1938 to the Cyrillic alphabet (used for Russian).

History: The Dargin who lived in the lowlands used to be part of a state called Qaitagh Umitsiate that became part of the Russian Empire in 1820. Those living in the mountains were members of independent **clans**. At first there were four of these clans, but by the beginning of the nineteenth century the number had grown to 10. The Dargin were finally taken over by Russia in 1844.

Culture: The mountain Dargin build stone houses with two or more floors, similar to those of other Daghestani groups. Those living in the lowlands have stone houses one or two levels high. The men wear a Circassian coat and felt cape; women wear long dresses, wide pants, and the *chikrit* head covering that is also worn by other Daghestanis.

The Dargin farm and breed sheep and cattle. They sometimes wander with their flocks and herds. They also have small businesses and make crafts.

DARGWA see DARGIN, KUBACHI.

DARIBI The Daribi are an **ethnic** group of about 10,000 people. They live in the high flatlands in south-central Papua New Guinea, near the Purari River. They speak their own native language. They do not have a particular religious belief, but do fear ghosts. Their main crop is the sweet potato, which they grow in the

Daribi

rich soil that once was lava from nearby volcanoes. They cut and burn the natural growth to prepare their fields for planting (slash-and-burn agriculture).

DAROOD A **clan** of the SOMALI in Somalia.

DASHAN see KACHIN.

DASNAYIS see ARMENIANS, IRAQIS, KURDS.

DASSA A group among the YORUBA in Benin.

DASSANETCH (also called Geleba, Merille, Reshevat) The Dassanetch are an **ethnic** group of about 40,000 people. They live north of Lake Turkana in southern Gemu Gofa Province, Ethiopia. Their language is part of the eastern Cushitic group. They practice their traditional religion.

The Dassanetch are farmers whose main crop is sorghum. They also raise cattle. In their society people are given honor and power according to their age and their generation.

DAUR (also called Dayur) The Daur are an **ethnic** group that lives in Heilongjiang Province in Inner Mongolia and Xinjiang Region in northern China. Experts estimate that there are 130,000 Daur.

Language: They speak Mongolian, which is an extremely old language. In fact, it is similar to Mongolian writings that go back to the thirteenth century. Since the Daur live in three areas, there are three slightly different versions of their language. During the Qing **dynasty** (1644–1911) they used Manchurian script for their writings as well. Since the 1910s they have changed to the Chinese script.

Religion and culture: Some Daur practice the Tibetan Buddhist religion. Most, however, have maintained their traditional religion, which is based on magic.

In the past they lived by wandering through the woods to hunt and to herd their flocks. Now they work more in farming, logging, hunting, raising animals, and breeding horses. Most Daur villages are made up of members of large extended families. People who have the same family name are not allowed to marry one another.

DAURAWA A group among the HAUSA of northern Nigeria.

DA VACH see HRE.

DAYAK Dayak is a general name for a number of **ethnic** groups that live on the island of Kalimantan (also called Borneo). This island is shared by the countries Indonesia and Malaysia. Experts believe that there are about two million of them.

The Dayak have maintained their traditional religious beliefs. Most live by farming rice, fishing, hunting, and gathering wild food and other products. Farmers prepare their fields for planting by first cutting and burning any natural growth (slash-and-burn agriculture). When the fields get worn out, they create new ones nearby.

Dayak

A Dayak man in Kalimantan (also called Borneo), Indonesia, wearing a ceremonial decoration on his head

Top: A Dayak woman near her home in Kalimantan (also called Borneo), Indonesia

Bottom: Dayak women wearing their festive clothes in Kalimantan

Sea Dayak: The IBAN, or Sea Dayak, are the most well-known Dayak group. They do not actually live on the sea but rather in the hills not far from the coast. Their name, Sea Dayak, was given to them by the DUTCH in the midnineteenth century. It comes from their reputation as cruel pirates during that time. There are over 400,000 Sea Dayak.

They speak a Malay **dialect**. Their religion includes special ceremonies they perform when they grow and harvest rice. Their supreme god, Sengalang Burong, has the form of a hawk and is connected to **headhunting**. The Iban worship the dead, which is common in traditional Indonesian religions.

The Iban gave up their practice of headhunting only after World War II. However, they still fight wars against neighboring people. They also often kidnap women and children from the peoples around them and turn them into slaves. The Indonesian government and Christian **missionaries** have been trying to get the Iban to stop these practices, with some success.

The Sea Dayak are growing and selling more and more rubber. Even so, rice has remained an important crop for eating, sharing, selling, and also for religious reasons. Young men sometimes move to other islands to earn more money. When they do, they still maintain strong ties to their villages and usually return home.

Land Dayak: Land Dayak, or BIDAYUH, is a general name for many small groups that practice their traditional religions in the Malaysian province of Sarawak and in West Kalimantan. There are about 550,000 Land Dayak. They are divided into many tribes, including the AUP, AYOU, BRANG, BUKAR, DESA, ENGKROH, ENGRAT, GROGO, JAGOI, KADUP, KUAP, LARA, LUNDU, MANYUKEI, MUALANG, SAMARAHAN, SARAMBAU, SAU, SEDUMAK, SELAKAN, SENNAH, SENTAH, SIBUNGO, SIDIN, SIGU, SIMPOKE, SINGGIE, and TAUP. Each group has its own native culture, but all share many aspects of their culture. All have been influenced by foreigners such as the MALAYS, JAVANESE, and CHINESE.

The Land Dayak have at times been taken advantage of by foreign groups. They claim that they were abused for years by others and see themselves as weak because of this. Unlike the Sea Dayak, the Land Dayak have been rather peaceful. However, some groups practiced ritual headhunting at one time. Today they farm for food but also grow rubber and coffee for sale. They also engage in iron-working and in trading for salt with people who live on the coast.

Maanyan Dayak: The MAANYAN DAYAK are a group that lives along the Patai River and the small streams that flow from it. There are about 35,000 of them. They are divided into four subgroups that speak the same language. Over 75 percent practice their traditional religion. This belief centers on the spirits of the dead and of nature. Another 20 percent are Christians. There is also a small Muslim community. They grow rice and fruit and also fish for food. Rubber and wood are important crops that they grow for sale.

Ngadju: NGADJU (also called Biadju, Oloh Kahayan) is the name used for a group of Dayak peoples who live along the rivers of southern Borneo. These groups include the BIADJU, BUKIT, DUSUN, KAHAYAN, KATINGAN, KOTAWARINGAN, LAWANGAN, MAANYAN, MURUNG, PATAI, SARUYAN, SIANG, SIONG, TABUYAN, TAMAN, and TAMOAN.

They grow rice, fish, and do some hunting. They also make baskets and pottery, weave cloth, and work iron. Other special crafts are tattooing and wood carving. The Ngadju speak a number of different languages and have many different religious beliefs. Most groups believe in a two-part god; the male part lives in the heavens, and the female part lives in the underworld.

Ot Danum Dayak: OT DANUM DAYAK is the name for the 100,000 people who live in central Borneo. They are divided into several tribes with very similar cultures. These include the DOHOI, PANANJOI, and TABAHOI. They speak dialects of the same language; however, speakers of one dialect do not necessarily understand another. They share the same religious beliefs. Their religion includes a legend that they believe comes from their gods and describes how they were divided into different tribes. They grow rice and prepare their fields for planting by first cutting and burning the natural growth (slash-and-burn agriculture). They are known for weaving baskets and other wicker items. They used to fight many wars. However, a peace ceremony that was held among all Dayak groups in the 1890s is very important to them for religious reasons. Some Ot Danum Dayak have converted to Christianity.

Because of the influence of people from coastal Malaysia, many Dayak have recently become Muslims. They call themselves "Orang Melayu" to show that they are different from the Dayak who worship many gods. They usually maintain their traditional languages.

Most Dayak live in permanent settlements. However, there are some groups who are **nomads**. They often have the word "Ot" at the beginning of their names. These include: Ot Danum Dayak, OT BALUI, OT MARUWEI, OT SIAU, and OT USU. Other wandering groups include the BUNGAN-BULIT, MELATUNG, PANJAWANT, PUNAN, and PUNAN KARAHL.

DAY-KUNDI A group among the HAZARA of Afghanistan.

DAYUR see DAUR.

DAZA (also called Dazagada) A **clan** of the TOUBOU of northern Chad.

DAZAGADA see DAZA.

DEBBA A group among the MABA of Chad.

DEI The 8,000 Dei live in Bomi County, Liberia. They speak a **dialect** of the Kru language, which is part of the Niger-Congo family. They were the first group to come into contact with the AMERICO-LIBERIANS. (see also LIBERIANS)

DEKKER A group among the MABA of Chad.

DELAWARE The Delaware are a Native North American group of about 3,000 that lived at first on the east coast of the United States. Today most live in Oklahoma, and about 10 percent live in southern Ontario, Canada, on the Moraviantown **Reserve**.

The history of the Delaware is much the same as that of other Native North American peoples. They were forced to move to Ohio after a number of violent conflicts with the BRITISH and the AMERICANS. After the War of 1812 they were forced onto an Indian **reservation**. They now live in the Federal Trust Area of the Delaware Indian Tribes of Western Oklahoma.

DEMONARA A group among the SOLORESE of eastern Indonesia.

DENE (also called Athapaskan) The Dene are one of the largest groups of native peoples in North America. There are 80,000 Dene. They live throughout the Yukon Territory, central Alaska, and the western part of the Northwest Territories in Canada.

Unlike many other Indian groups, the Dene have maintained their traditional way of life. Their language, called Athapaskan, is widely spoken today, even by the younger people. The Dene have been very successful in convincing the Canadian government to honor their claims to their native lands. The first native member of parliament in Canada was a Dene woman from Yukon Territory.

DENKYIRA The Denkyira are an Akan group that lives in the Western Region of Ghana. Before the Europeans came to the area, they had the most powerful state in the region. It was conquered by the ASHANTI in 1701.

DEORI The Deori are an **ethnic** group who live in Arunachal Pradesh and Assam, India. There are about 20,000 of them. They speak a language that is part of the Tibeto-Burman family.

The Deori are members of the MONGOL race and are one of the four groups that belong to the CHUTIA people. The Chutia set up self-rule areas in the upper region of Brahmaputra, India.

They practice the Hindu religion and also worship household gods. They never marry people who are in the same **clan**.

The Deori live near rivers and build large, tall houses facing them. More than 40 people can live in one house. They are farmers, and their main food is rice.

DESA An **ethnic** group that lives on the island of Kalimantan (also called Borneo) in Indonesia. (see also DAYAK)

DEUTSCHE see GERMANS.

DHANGAR The Dhangar are an **ethnic** group that lives in Jhapa, Biratnagar, Saptari, Mahottari, and Sarlahi, in Nepal. They speak Kurux, which is a Dravidian language. They write it using Devanagari.

They are mainly farmers, but they also raise cattle and fowl. They are skilled at making household tools out of bamboo.

DHANKA (also called Tadvi Bhil) The Dhanka are an **ethnic** group of about 255,000 people. They live in Panch Mahals, Broach, Baroda, and West Khandesh in the states of Gujarat, Maharashtra, and Rajasthan, in India. They speak the Bhili **dialect**, which is part of the Indo-Aryan language family. They worship a supreme god and also honor local gods.

The Dhanka who live on the plains work mostly at farming and various jobs in the forest. They collect many useful things from the forest, including gum, honey, leaves of trees for making country cigars, and wood to sell in other countries. Their main foods are rice and millet.

DHANUHAR see DHANWAR.

DHANWAR (also called Dhanuhar) The Dhanwar are an **ethnic** group of about 130,000 people. They live in the hills of Bilaspur in Madhya Pradesh and Maharashtra, India. Their language is part of the Indo-Aryan family.

The Dhanwar practice the Hindu religion. Their main gods are Thakur Deo, the god of agriculture, and Dulha Deo, the god of the family and the home.

DHIMAL (also called Maulik) The Dhimal are an **ethnic** group that numbers 15,000. They live in northern India and eastern Nepal. Their language is part of the Tibeto-Burman family. They work mostly at farming and herding animals. Some work in the large plantations where Darjeeling tea is grown.

DHUNDIA The Dhundia are a people who live in the state of Gujarat in western India. There are about 500,000 of them, mostly farmers.

DHURIA A group among the NAGESIA in northeast India.

DHURWA (call themselves Parja) The Dhurwa are an **ethnic** group of about 100,000 people. They live in Bastar District, Madhya Pradesh, India.

The Dhurwa are farmers. When their fields get worn out, they create new ones nearby. They also sell forest products. Some Dhurwa work as laborers in the local public works department which builds roads in the district.

The Dhurwa do not eat beef or other animals or plants to which they believe they are related. They also do not eat with or marry members of other tribes. Those Durwa who live in hard-to-reach villages in the interior part of the country have little contact with outsiders. Only members of the same clan live in these villages.

DIAN An **ethnic** group that lives in Burkina Faso and is related to the LOBI.

DIARI An Australian native group that lives in northeastern South Australia, near Lake Eyre. Hardly anybody can still speak their native language. They hunt and gather wild food and other materials. (see also AUSTRALIAN ABORIGINES)

DIAWONDO A small **ethnic** group that lives in Mali.

DIBONGIYA see CHUTIA.

DIDA The Dida are an **ethnic** group of about 100,000 that lives in the south central part of the Ivory Coast. They speak a language of the Kru group of the Niger-Congo family. They maintain their traditional religion. Many are supporters of the movement of William Wade Harris, who was an African Christian prophet in the twentieth century.

The Dida never had a central government; however, they did try to prevent the FRENCH from controlling them. Even so, they came under French rule after World War I. After World War II they began to grow crops such as coffee and cocoa to sell. In the late 1950s there were ethnic tensions between the Dida and the DYULA and BAULE who had moved into the area.

DIDAYI The Didayi are a small group of about 3,000 people. They live in the state of Orissa in India. They speak the Munda language, which belongs to the South-Asiatic family. They are farmers.

DIDINGA The Didinga are a group that lives in southwest Sudan, south of the Toposa hills. Experts estimate that there are about 80,000 of them. They speak an eastern Sudanic language. They both farm and herd cattle. Most follow local African beliefs.

DIDO (call themselves Avar, Tsez) The Dido are an **ethnic** group that lives in the mountains of northwest Daghestan. There are over 7,000 of them. They are Sunni Muslims of the Shafi'i school. It seems that they became Muslims in about the sixteenth century. Their language is part of the Avar-Andi-Dido group of the North Caucasian family. It has no written form; the Dido use Avarian for writing.

The Dido are now in the process of being absorbed by the AVAR group. Today they call themselves both Avar and Tsez.

The Dido are sheep-herders. They build tall stone houses with a two-part roof. The style of their houses is like that of the GEORGIANS. Dido women wear large earrings that reach their shoulders.

DIGARU see MISHMI.

DIGIL A **clan** among the SOMALI of Somalia.

DIGO A group among the MIJIKENDA of Kenya.

DIGOR see OSSET.

DIHARIA (also called Kisan Korwa) A group among the KORWA of northeastern India.

DIJIOKO A group among the SARA of southern Chad.

DIMA see DIME.

DIMASA see BORO-KACHARI.

DIMASA-KACHARI The Dimasa-Karachi are an **ethnic** group of about 100,000 people. They are found in the North Kachar Hill District in Assam, India. Their language is part of the Tibeto-Burman family.

The Dimasa-Kachari belong to the Boro grouping of peoples, which includes the BORO-KACHARI, MECH, RABHA, LALUNG, and KOCH of Assam. Experts believe that the Dimasa-Kachari once lived in western China, near where the Yangtze and Hwang rivers begin. They practice the Hindu religion.

They are mostly farmers who prepare their fields for planting by first cutting and burning the natural growth (slash-and-burn agriculture). Dimasa who live on the flatlands grow their rice in wet fields.

DIME (also called Dima) The Dime are a small **ethnic** group of a few thousand people. They live west of the Mago River in central Gemu Gofa Province, Ethiopia. Their language is part of the Omotic group. They practice their traditional religions. The Dime population has grown smaller because of widespread disease and because many have moved out of the area.

The Dime farm by cutting terraces into the hillside to create fields. They live in permanent settlements in stone houses. Those living in the lowlands also raise cattle.

DINDE A group among the SARA of southern Chad.

DINKA The Dinka are a people who live in southern Sudan. There are about three million Dinka, which is about 10 percent of the total population of the country. They are the largest **ethnic** group in southern Sudan, making up 40 percent of the people in that area. Some Dinka also live in Ethiopia and Kenya.

Dinka

The Dinka speak an Eastern Sudanic language. The majority follow the traditional Dinka religion. Others have become Christians. The Dinka raise cattle, which are important in their religion. They also trade cattle instead of using money. The Dinka are important to the modern history of Sudan. It was a Dinka, John Garang, who led the southern people of Sudan in a long and bloody war against the Muslim-controlled Sudanese government. (see also SUDANESE)

DIOLA (also called Jola) The Diola are an **ethnic** group that lives in Senegal, in the area where the Casamance River flows into the Atlantic Ocean. There are about 800,000 Diola, which is nine percent of the Senegalese population. They also live in the Fomi areas south of Bitang Bolon in nearby Gambia, where they make up 10 percent of the population, or 120,000 people. They speak Diola, one of the six official languages in Senegal. Most Diola are Christians, although there are a few Muslims also scattered among them. The Diola never had their own central government. When the FRENCH controlled Senegal and the BRITISH ruled Gambia, many

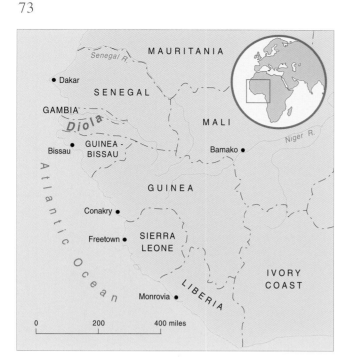

Diola

Diola moved to the cities. Their traditional culture absorbed many Western ways, including modern education, Christianity, and Islam.

Since Senegal has become independent, the Diola have been active in politics. They have been leaders in a movement of local people that claims that the government is ignoring their region. (Their province is separated from the rest of Senegal by the state of Gambia.) Since the early 1980s these protests have sometimes become violent.

The BAINOUK and the BALANTE are subgroups of the Diola. (see GAMBIANS, SENEGALESE)

DIONGOR see DIONKOR.

DIONKOR (also called Diongor) An **ethnic** group that lives in central Chad. They number about 25,000. The Dionkor speak a language that belongs to the Chadic group of the Afro-Asiatic family and they are closely related to the HADJERAY.

DIR A **clan** among the SOMALI of Somalia.

DIRI The Diri are an **ethnic** group of about 50,000 that lives in the area of Dir, in north Pakistan. They speak a number of similar **dialects**. The main one is Bashkarik, which has become the name for the entire group of dialects. It is part of the Dardic group of Indo-Aryan languages. It has no written form; Urdu is used by the Diri for writing and education. They also use the Pashto language of Paskistan when speaking to people who are not Deri. They are Sunni Muslims of the Hanafi school.

The Deri are farmers who live in permanent settlements. Since the seventeenth century they have been ruled by a family of the Akhund-Khel Pashtun **clan**. This clan has two parts: the higher, ruling class, and the lower level, which governs the rest of the Deri. Each of the higher-class clan members owns a large land area. All those living on this land are **serfs** of the head of the ruling family in their area.

DIVARA see HALE PAIKA.

DIVEHI see MALDIVIANS.

DIZI (also called Dizu) The Dizi are an **ethnic** group of about 25,000 that lives in the Maji Mountains in southern Kefa Province, Ethiopia. They follow their traditional religious beliefs.

After the Dizi area became part of the Ethiopian Empire in 1898, it was a center for trade in ivory, slaves, and weapons.

DIZU see DIZI.

DJALLONKE see YALUNKA.

DJAMBI MALAY see BATIN.

DJANE A **clan** of the DJOHEINA of Chad.

DJEM One of the groups among the MABA of Chad.

DJERMA (also called Dyerma, Zerma, Zarma) The Djerma are a people related to the SONGHAI. They live in the valley of the Niger River, from Djenne in Mali to Gaya in Niger. They number two million people and form 22 percent of the population of Niger. There are also some Djerma in the Nikki-Kandi area of Benin. They speak Djerma and most are Muslims.

During the nineteenth century they fought a war with the FULANI people. Although the Djerma lost a large portion of their lands in this war, their identity as a people became stronger. By the end of that century they were able to win back their territory from the Fulani.

Before the Europeans ruled in Africa, the Djerma lived in small village-states that had some self-rule. They did not try to prevent the FRENCH from taking over their area. During French rule and after, many Djerma moved to Ghana and the Ivory Coast to find work. (see also NIGERIANS)

A Djerma woman wearing a traditional headdress

DJIBOUTIANS The Djiboutians are the people of about 450,000 who live in the African country of Djibouti. This country used to be the FRENCH territory of the AFAR and ISSA peoples in East Africa. The official languages of the country are Arabic and French. Most of the people are Muslims.

The Djiboutians are made up of four main groups: Afar, Issa, ARABS (mostly YEMENIS), and Europeans. Most of the people live in or near the capital city, Djibouti, and work for the government or for foreign companies. In the past Djiboutians were mainly farmers and cattle-herders.

Peoples: Djibouti has suffered from continual fights and struggles among its different groups. The Issa, who make up almost 50 percent of the population, are closely related to the SOMALI. By contrast, the Afar, who make up 35 percent of the population, are related to the Afar, a much larger group that lives mostly in Ethiopia. Both Somalia and Ethiopia have tried to claim parts of Djibouti for themselves (they have since given up these claims).

The severe climate also adds to the struggle between peoples. Since 90 percent of the country is harsh desert, everybody must share the 10 percent of cattle-grazing land that remains. In addition, because Djibouti has an important location on the Horn of Africa, and because of its valuable port at the entrance to the Red Sea, different groups have wanted to control it. When the FRENCH controlled the area, they showed favoritism toward the Afar.

History: The French pushed into the region in 1862, and Djibouti came fully under French control in 1900. The French Foreign Legion was stationed there because of Djibouti's important location in Africa. The French did not want to let go of this valuable African property; Djibouti was the last African nation to become independent in 1977. French and other European influences remain strong in the country.

The government of Djibouti was able to keep the main **ethnic** groups from fighting by passing certain laws. These include a rule that the nation's president must come from the Issa people, and the prime minister must be an Afar.

Economy: Almost 70 percent of the working people in Djibouti have jobs that provide services to the French and other Europeans who live in the country. Poor development, lack of water, and conflicts among peoples throughout the Horn of Africa region all slow down the economy. These problems also contribute to making the young country of Djibouti weaker and less stable.

DJIMINI The Djimini are an **ethnic** group that lives in the Ivory Coast, in the Dabakala region, between the Comoe and Nzi rivers. This is on the southern edge of Senufo territory. Their language is close to that of the SENUFO people. They are mostly Muslims, but many also practice their traditional religion or Christianity.

DJOHEINA The Djoheina are a group of clans of **seminomads** who live in Chad. They came from the Nile River valley in Sudan between the fourteenth and nineteenth centuries. There are about 350,000 of them divided into several clans. The most important clan is the MISIRIE (meaning "Egyptians"), who live in Ouadai Region.

Until recently the Misirie fought against other groups in the area. Many joined small armies that worked against Chad's first president, Ngarta Tombalaye.

Other clans include: the SALAMAT ARABS, who live between the Chari River and Oudai; the RIGEZAT, who are spread from Oudai Region to Sudan's Darfur Region; the OULED RACHID, in the Batha Valley and in the southern Baguirmi area; the OULED HEMAT, who are found all over the eastern part of the country; the DJANE; and the KHOZZAM. (see also CHADIANS)

DLAMINI A clan of the SWAZI of Swaziland.

DOBRUJAN TATAR see CRIMEAN TATARS.

DOBU ISLANDERS The Dobu Islanders are an **ethnic** group that lives on Dobu Island and islands near the southeastern coast of Papua New Guinea. There are about 10,000 of them. They speak a local native language that is also spoken by a few more thousand people on other islands.

Many Dobu have adopted Christianity, and village churches are important places in their community. The Dobu also believe in many traditional **myths**, and magic spells.

The main crop of the Dobu is yams. They prepare their fields for farming by first cutting and burning the natural growth (slash-and-burn agriculture). When a field gets worn out, they create a new one nearby.

DODOTH The Dodoth are a people who live in the northeast part of Uganda. They number a few tens of thousand. Their language belongs to the Eastern Sudanic group of the Nilo-Saharan family. It is much like the languages of the KARAMOJONG and TESO peoples.

The Dodoth used to be part of the KARAMOJONG and think of them as closely related. They believe in only one god, Akuj, who is far away and does not take an interest in their everyday life. Today many have become Christians, and some are also Muslims.

The Dodoth are cattle-herders. Cattle are at the center of their culture and social life. They use cattle, rather than money, to measure how much wealth each person has. These animals are also exchanged when two groups agree to unite and as part of marriage arrangements. Farming is not very important to the Dodoth.

The Dodoth live in scattered settlements. Their families are made up of **clans**. Males are leaders in the clans, and inheritances are passed from father to son. Traditionally, Dodoth only married people from outside their own clan. The men are arranged in groups according to their age. The oldest group is the "elders," who are given the most honor and respect. They also have the most power in the community. Each time a man moves up to a new age level, he is honored with a special ceremony. When the BRITISH ruled the area, they introduced chiefs as leaders of the Dodoth. (see also KARAMOJONG)

DOGHOSIÉ   An **ethnic** group that lives in southwest Burkina Faso.

DOGON   The Dogon are an **ethnic** group that lives in the African country of Mali and across the border in Burkina Faso. They number 470,000 in Mali and 140,000 in Burkina Faso. Their home is on the mountain cliffs of Bandiagra, which are east of Mopti. They speak their own language, called Dogon. Most practice traditional religions but are slowly converting to Islam.

At the beginning of the fourteenth century the Dogon wanted to escape from conquerors who were trying to force them to convert to Islam. They therefore built their villages on hard-to-reach mountain cliffs. They developed their own special method of farming, which is suited to the challenges of the land around them. They are also famous for their art; many people think it is the best in West Africa.

When Mali was becoming independent, the Dogon formed their own political party. However, they did not take a major part in the country's politics. (see also MALIANS)

DOG RIB   The Dog Rib are a Native North American group. They live in five communities in the Northwest Territories, Canada, between Great Slave Lake and Great Bear Lake. Today there are only about 3,000 of them. Their language belongs to the Athapaskan group, which is part of the Na-Dene family.

Many still practice their traditional way of earning a living, which is to hunt and trap animals.

DOHOI   An **ethnic** group that lives in the south of Kalimantan Island (also called Borneo) in Indonesia. (see also DAYAK)

DOLAGO   An **ethnic** group that lives in the mountains in the center area of the island of Sulawesi (also called Celebes) in Indonesia. (see also TORADJA)

DOLGAN   (call themselves Tya-Kikhi, Sakha) The Dolgan are the main people in Taymyr Autonomous Province of Yakutia, located at the far northeastern edge of the Russian Federation. Their home is in the extremely cold region north of the Arctic Circle. There are about 5,500 of them. They originally come from several **clans** of the EVENKI people. They speak a language which is part of the Turkic group of the Altaic family. It is written in a Cyrillic alphabet that they adopted from the YAKUT people. They maintain their traditional religion, which is based on magic.

DOMETE   see OMETO.

Dolgan

DOMINICA ISLANDERS The Dominica Islanders are the people of the Commonwealth of Dominica in the Caribbean Sea, an independent state located in the Windward Islands. There are about 85,000 Dominica Islanders. English is the main language, and a local French **dialect** is also spoken. Almost all are Roman Catholics.

Most Dominica Islanders originally came from African slaves whom the French brought to the island to work on their large coffee and sugar plantations. However, some descend from the CARIB Indian people who have always lived on the island. The Carib have been able to hold onto their traditional lifestyle and identity as a people by living in a separate area.

The FRENCH first took control of the island in 1727. They gave it to the BRITISH in 1763. Dominica became independent in 1978.

The island's income comes from farming and tourism. Hurricanes damage the island's plantations from time to time, especially the banana crop, which is the island's main product.

DOMINICANS The Dominicans are the people of the Dominican Republic. This country is made up of the eastern two-thirds of the island of Hispaniola (the western third of the island is Haiti). There are over eight million Dominicans. Today's Dominicans are a mix of the Spanish settlers who came to the island in the fifteenth century and the African slaves whom they brought with them. They Spanish also absorbed other groups who moved to the island from other Spanish-ruled areas, such as the Canary Islands. The Dominicans speak Spanish.

Religion: Most Dominicans are Roman Catholics. Some have recently become evangelical Protestants who are trying to spread their religion, particularly on eastern Samana peninsula. Dominicans who live in rural areas usually do not go to church often. Compared to other Latin American countries, there are few churches in rural areas.

History: Christopher Columbus founded his first settlements in the "New World" on this island. When he arrived, he found many Tainos people living there. This native group was part of the ARAWAK peoples that lived all over the islands in the region. Fewer than 50 years after Columbus' arrival, almost all of the Tainos were dead. Some died from hunger or diseases brought by the Europeans that they were not used to. Others were killed, were worked to death, or committed suicide. As the Tainos died off, SPANIARDS and their African slaves moved onto the island.

The Dominicans have fought many wars and gone through many periods when Europeans ruled their country. Columbus moved his governing center for Hispaniola to Santo Domingo in 1496. For one generation Hispaniola was the center of the new Spanish empire in the New World. However, all of its gold mines had been emptied by the mid-1500s. For several hundred years after that few people lived there, and there was almost no development.

The Dominican Republic gained its independence from Spain in 1821. It was attacked and occupied by Haiti almost immediately. The HAITIANS ruled for 22 years. Spain took over the island again in 1861. The islanders fought a second War of the Restoration to regain their independence in 1865. Since the Dominican Republic was a weak country, its government asked the United States for help, and even to take control of the island in 1870. In fact, the United States did rule the Dominican Republic at several points during the last century. From 1916 to 1924 the U.S. Army governed the island. In 1965 the U.S. Marines went there to set up a friendly government.

Between 1930 and 1961 the country was ruled by an army dictator, General Rafael Trujillo. He built up the capital city, Santo Domingo, very rapidly. For a while he even changed the name of the city to his own, Ciudad Trujillo. He forced people to live in rural areas that he had chosen, especially near the border with Haiti. This caused so much tension that over 10,000 Haitians who had moved to the area without permission were killed in 1937. Trujillo was assassinated, and Juan Balaguer became president. He has ruled the country for most of the last 30 years.

The number of Dominicans has grown rapidly in the twentieth century. Many have moved to or near Santo Domingo. The largest city used to be Santiago, but now Santo Domingo has over three million people, which is nearly half of the country's total population (and five times more than Santiago). About a million Dominicans have left the island. They have moved mostly to the United States and Venezuela. Dominicans in the U.S. have formed their own neighborhood communities in cities such as New York.

Culture: In rural areas most Dominicans live in simple houses near unpaved roads. They usually build their houses from the wood of the local "royal palm" tree. The roof is also made from woven palm leaves. Most families have their own small gardens and grow the food they need throughout the year. Few homes in rural areas have running water. Children are often seen bringing home pails of water on the back of a donkey.

In cities, houses are usually made of cement-block walls with metal roofs. In Santo Domingo especially, different people live extremely different lifestyles. It has beautiful, wealthy neighborhoods and also crowded, rundown settlements that the homeless have set up.

DOMPU (call themselves Dou Dompu) The Dompu are the main **ethnic** group that lives on a strip of land in the center of the island of Sumbawa, Indonesia. There are about 25,000 of them, and almost all practice the Muslim religion. They speak Biman, which belongs to the Malayo-Polynesian family. Most are farmers who grow rice.

DON COSSACKS see UKRAINIANS.

DONDO I An **ethnic** group in Zimbabwe.

DONDO II An **ethnic** group that lives in the Buenza Region of the Republic of Congo. The Dondo are related to the KONGO people. (see also CONGOLESE [CONGO (ZAIRE)].

DONG (also called Tong, Tung, Tong-chia; call themselves Kam) The Dong live mainly in Guizhou, Hunan, and Guanxi provinces of southwest China. There are about 2.6 million of them. They first appeared in China during the Sung **dynasty**, which ruled from 960 to 1127. They soon moved south, possibly because of invasions by the Mongols.

Language: Their language is part of the Zhuang-Dong group of the language family that is common in southwest China. They borrowed many words from the HAN CHINESE and also their traditional way of writing using picture symbols. In 1958 the Chinese government gave them their own writing system using the Roman alphabet (used for English).

The Dong live mostly by farming and harvesting forest products. Their major crops include rice, wheat, corn, tobacco, and cotton. They build their houses about the same as their

Dong

neighbors, the YAO and MIAO. Their houses have several levels and are of medium height. The Dong have pagodalike drum towers in the centers of most of their villages. These towers are important social gathering places. The Dong believe in many gods.

DONGGALA An **ethnic** group that lives in the mountains of the center area of the island of Sulawesi (also called Celebes) in Indonesia. (see also TORADJA)

DONGGO (call themselves Dou Donggo) The Donggo are an **ethnic** group that lives in six mountain villages in the eastern part of the island of Sumbawa, Indonesia. There are about 15,000 of them who speak a **dialect** of Biman. They have maintained their traditional religion, which is based on **ancestor worship**. Their religious rituals center around holy stones where they believe their gods meet.

The Donggo grow rice and also hunt wild boar and birds. The DUTCH also introduced coffee as a cash crop. They prepare their fields for planting by first cutting and burning the natural growth (slash-and-burn agriculture).

DONGOLAWI see JABELAWI.

DONGOLAWIN A group among the NUBIANS of Sudan.

DONGXIANG (also called Tonghsiang; call themselves Sang) The Dongxiang live mostly in southwest Gansu Province of northwest China. There are about 400,000 of them. Nobody is sure exactly where they come from. Many experts believe that they were originally MONGOLIANS who were converted to Sunni Islam by Muslim neighbors. Since the other Mongolians were Buddhists, they saw the Dongxiang as traitors to their religion. The Donxiang were therefore forced to move to their present home. They have also been called "Mongolian Hui Hui," which means Mongolian Muslims.

Their language is part of the Mongolian family. However, they have borrowed a great deal from Chinese as well. Many Donxiang speak Chinese, and most use it for writing.

Most Dongxiang are Muslims, and Islam has a great influence on their daily life. They are farmers who grow mainly potatoes, wheat, and barley. Their way of life and culture have much in common with their neighbors, the HUI people, who are also Muslims.

DORLA The Dorla are an **ethnic** group that lives in various parts of Madhya Pradesh, India. There are about 50,000 of them. They are related to the KOYA people, who also live in the area. They speak Dorla, a **dialect** of Koya, which belongs to the Dravidian family. They maintain their traditional religions but are also Hindu.

Experts believe that the name "Dorla" comes from the word *doralu,* which means chieftains or important people. They are experts at archery. Their main work is farming and gathering food from their area. They prepare their fields for farming by first cutting and burning the natural growth (slash-and-burn agriculture).

DORLA SATAM see KOYA.

DOROBO see NDOROBO.

DOROSIE (also called Dorobe) see LOBI.

DORZE The Dorze are an **ethnic** group that lives west of Lake Abaya in the eastern Gemu Gofa Province, Ethiopia. There are about 50,000 of them. Their language is part of the Omotic group. They practice their traditional religions. The Dorze used to farm by cutting many terraces into the hillsides to create fields. They also earned a living as merchants, soldiers for hire, and workers in nearby states.

Traditionally, their society and politics were based on **clans**. Each male competed with the other males for his status in the community. Some leaders were elected. Once the Dorze became part of the Ethiopian Empire, they moved to cities and became more modern. Today more than half live in cities and towns.

DOU BIMA see BIMANESE.

DOU DOMPU see DOMPU.

DOU DONGGO see DONGGO.

DOU HAWU see SAYUNESE.

DOUKHOBORS see CANADIANS.

DRUZE (also called Durua; call themselves Muwahhidun, Unitarists) The Druze are an **ethnic** and religious group that is scattered in communities in Lebanon, Syria, and Israel. There are also smaller groups of Druze in Jordan, West Africa, the United States, Canada, and Latin America. Over the centuries the Druze have developed into a separate Arabic-speaking ethnic group. They have their own special culture based on their strong loyalty to one another, their religion, and their skill at fighting.

Religion: The Druze practice an unusual secret religion. It first appeared in the eleventh century, when a small group broke off from the Shi'ite Isma'ili sect of Islam. Its first religious leader was ad-Darazi. He declared that the ruling sultan of the Fatamid **dynasty**, al-Hakim, was actually God born into a human body.

Baba al-din al-Muqtana later shaped the religion into its traditional form. He created its special collection of holy letters. Soon after, the Druze became a closed community and began to keep their beliefs secret. The most hidden beliefs are known only to a select group called the *uqqal.* The rest of the Druze, the *juhhal,* do not know all

that there is to know about their own religion. However, all followers believe that people are regularly reborn as other people after they die. The Druze religion seems to have some traces of Gnostic and other ancient religions. The Druze place a great deal of importance on being helpful and truthful toward other Druze. Druze women generally enjoy greater freedom than Muslim women.

History: Al-Hakim tried to spread his new religion in Egypt, but he failed. The Druze were treated harshly there, and they fled to Syria. They were able to survive in hard-to-reach mountain villages in Syria, near Mount Hermon, Mount Lebanon, the Matn, and Shouf. There were also Maronite Christians living in these areas. They and the Muslims both **persecuted** the Druze.

In the seventeenth century many Druze moved to Galilee and Mount Carmel in Palestine (now called Israel). Their major holy places are

A Druze in his traditional clothes

Hasbaya in Lebanon and the grave of their prophet, Shueib (Jethro, Moses's father-in-law), in Galilee.

From time to time the Druze have had to organize themselves to fight against outsiders. There has also been some fighting among themselves. In the sixteenth century the Druze supported the Ottomans who were taking over their area. As a result, they were rewarded with the right to rule themselves under the Druze Ma'anid **dynasty** (1517–1697). At times other Druze leaders tried to gain independence from the Ma'anids. When the Ma'anid dynasty ended, the Druze revolted against the Turkish government from time to time. From the late seventeenth until the early nineteenth century the Shihabi Dynasty led the Druze. During this period the Maronites often worked as **serfs** for the Druze. This led to later tensions between the two groups. The Druze leader Bashir II (1788–1840) won independence from the Ottoman Empire for a short while.

However, the Druze became weaker from fighting among themselves. At the same time, the Maronites grew stronger, and some Druze converted to their Christian religion. In 1841 a civil war broke out between the two groups. In 1860 the Christians revolted and demanded more rights to the land in the Christian-Druze Shouf area. They were cruelly crushed by the Druze, and 10,000 Christians were murdered. France sent in soldiers to protect the Christians, and forced the Ottoman Empire to create an area of some self-rule, called Christian Mount Lebanon. The Druze were put down, and their power over the area was broken. Half of them left for the Hawran region in southern Syria. They drove out the people they found there and continued to rule themselves.

Lebanon: When the Ottoman Empire was broken apart after World War I, the Druze found

Druze religious leaders

themselves in three different countries. They have never tried to create a state of their own. Today as many as 200,000 Druze live in Lebanon. They joined there with the PALESTINIANS in the 1975 civil war and were defeated after the Syrians became involved. When the Israelis withdrew from the Shouf region in 1983, many Druze and Maronites were murdered.

Syria: The greatest number of Druze live in Syria (300,000, or 3.5 percent of the country's population). In 1920 the French gave Jabal al Duruz (the Druze Mountain) to the Druze as a separate state. It was led by the al-Atrash family. Even so, the Druze joined with the Arabs in revolting against the French. The revolt was put down by the French in 1925–27. In the 1930s the Druze lands finally became part of Syria. Syria did not invest in developing the Druze area. However, Druze young men have had great success in Syria's army.

Israel: The 70,000 Druze in Israel live mostly in Galilee and on Mount Carmel. They serve in the army and police force of Israel. Because they support the JEWS in this way, they are usually treated better than the Muslim and Christian ARABS. Even so, some of the younger Druze see themselves more as Arabs of the Druze religion. (see also ISRAELIS, LEBANESE, PALESTINIANS, SYRIANS)

DUAISH A group among the MAURES of Mauritania.

DUALA The Duala are an **ethnic** group of over 100,000 who live on the coast of Cameroon. They speak Duala, which is part of the Bantu group of the Niger-Congo family. Most were converted to Christianity by **missionaries**. The missionaries used Duala to speak to all the peoples along the coast of Cameroon. Before the Europeans ruled in Africa, the Duala were involved in selling other Africans as slaves to them.

In the late nineteenth century the Duala king signed a treaty with Germany. This agreement allowed the Germans to control all of Cameroon. After World War I Duala territory came under French rule. During those years the Duala sold some of their lands to the BAMILEKE people and to Europeans. They have gradually become poorer and lost power in the region.

DUANE An **ethnic** group that lives in Vietnam and Laos. Experts group them together with the JEH, MENAM, NOAR, and SAYAN peoples. Their language belongs to the Mon-Khmer family.

DUBLA The Dubla are an **ethnic** group of 500,000 people. They live in India in the states of Gujarat, Goa, Karnataka, and Maharashtra, and in the territory of Daman and Diu. They speak a language related to Bhili, which is part of the Indo-Aryan family. Most practice the Hindu religion, but some are Christian or Muslim.

The Dubla are extremely poor. They were attacked for years by Rajput and other criminals, and forced to pay extremely high taxes. They fell into such debt that they sold themselves to work in fields as **serfs**. They were often sold by one landowner to another. Because of their problems, India's great leader, Mahatma Ghandi, did away with the practice of being a serf in 1923. Most Dubla now receive salaries to work on the farms of others.

DUFF ISLANDERS The Duff Islanders were an **ethnic** group that spoke Polynesian. There are now none of them alive. They lived on a chain of small volcanic islands called the Solomons; the main island is Taumako.

DUGBATANG see ATA MANOBO.

DUKKAWA An **ethnic** group of about 100,000 in Kebbi State of Nigeria. The language is part of the Niger-Congo family. They keep their traditional religion but some are Muslim. They are farmers and hunters.

DULANGON see COTABATO MANOBO.

DUMA A group among the KARANGA of Zimbabwe.

DUMBUSEYA The Dumbuseya are a group that lives in the Zwishaware region of Zimbabwe. They speak the Shona language. They seem to have originally come from SHONA people who were running away from the NGUNI in the 1830s.

DUNGAN see HUI.

DUONG A group among the SEMANG of Malaysia.

DURRANI A group among the PASHTUN in Afghanistan.

DURU An **ethnic** group of 60,000 that lives in the North Province of Cameroon in the plains areas. Their language, which is part of the Niger-Congo family, is widely spoken by many ethnic groups in Cameroon. They maintain their traditional religion.

DURUMA A group among the MIJIKENDA of eastern Kenya.

DURUZ see DRUZE.

DUSHMAN-ZIARI One of the four tribes that make up the MAMASAN in south-central Iran.

DUSUN (call themselves Tuhun Ngaavi, Kadazan) The Dusun are a people who live in the Malaysian province of Sabah on the island of Kalimantan (also called Borneo). There are about 400,000 of them. Their language is part of the Malayo-Polynesian family. They continue to practice their traditional religion, even though the Malaysian government encourages Islam.

The Dusun have had much contact with CHINESE, INDIANS, and MALAYS, who have come as traders to the island for over 2,000 years. They also have been ruled by a number of different countries that have all left their mark on Dusun culture. These include: the Buddhist state of Srivijaya, the Hindu state of Majapahit, Catholic Portugal, and Protestant Britain. Today the Malaysian government is pushing its culture and Muslim religion on the Dusun.

The Dusun mainly farm rice. They use varied techniques depending on the growing conditions in different parts of the island. They also raise water buffalo, pigs, chickens, and ducks.

DUTCH (call themselves Netherlanders) The 16 million Dutch live in the Netherlands (Holland), one of the most crowded countries in the world.

Flowers in a Dutch town in the Netherlands

Language: Dutch is a West Germanic language that comes from the **dialect** of Holland. It contains clear traces of the Flemish and Brabantine languages. Dutch is spoken by over 20 million people, including the FLEMINGS of Belgium. The FRISIANS, who live in the northern Netherlands, speak a separate language.

Religion and peoples: While the Dutch are traditionally made up of one **ethnic** group, they practice several religions. Protestants used to be who occupied the Netherlands during World War II. In recent years other groups have settled in the Netherlands. They include: SPANIARDS, PORTUGUESE, TURKS, INDONESIANS, MOROCCANS, SURINAMESE, and people from netherlands antilles. They now make up six percent of the population of the Netherlands.

Regions: The lives of the Dutch vary depending on the area of the Netherlands they live in. For example, those who live in Holland

A Dutch woman near a street-organ

the largest religious group, though divided into many smaller churches and sects. There are now more Catholics (34 percent) than Protestants (25 percent). Over a third are not really connected to any religion.

For many years Huguenots and JEWS were leading minority groups in the Netherlands. They had settled there to escape religious **persecution**. Most of the Jews were killed by the GERMANS proper have the most developed economy and culture. The city of Amsterdam is very open and modern; Zealand and Overijssel are rather traditional.

History: The Dutch originally came from three West Germanic peoples: the Frisians, Franks, and Saxons. In the eighth century they adopted Christianity. The Dutch lived as **serfs** in a number of farming villages during the time of the

Holy Roman Empire. They were absorbed into the Burgundians' growing territories in the fifteenth century. Under Habsburg rule they suffered from religious persecution of Protestants, tight government control, and extremely high taxes. This led them to stage a successful revolt. The United Provinces, the first Dutch government, came into being in 1579.

The Dutch grew wealthy with merchant ships that sailed throughout Scandinavia. They also

been under Spanish rule and had adopted the Catholic religion. Since then, a physical border between the Catholics and the Protestants has remained where the Rhine and Meuse rivers begin.

By the end of the seventeenth century the Dutch had lost their position as a great world power. Their economy grew again in the nineteenth century, and Catholics were allowed to practice their religion freely. However, these developments led to major social tensions within the country. The Dutch

Two Dutchmen carrying cheese at a cheese exhibition

profited from trade routes in the Atlantic Ocean that connected them to the East and West Indies. Wealthy, upper-class Flemish settlers helped make the seventeenth century the "Golden Age" for Holland. Art, sciences, and open-minded philosophies blossomed. At the same time, their Calvinist religion was very closed and strict.

The southern Dutch provinces became part of the Netherlands in 1648. Up until then they had

became divided into four "pillars"—subgroups that each had its own political party, schools, trade unions, media, etc. They are: Protestants, Catholics, liberals, and socialists. Members of each pillar have little to do with one another. Each pillar used to send its leaders to negotiate with the others when making decisions and dividing up the country's resources. This special power-sharing system existed until the 1960s.

In the 1970s about 500,000 foreign workers arrived in the Netherlands. This created many new minority groups. Racial hatred has *not* appeared among the Dutch as it has in other European countries. However, there is also very little integration of foreigners into Dutch society.

DUWABLAS A group among the KUBU on the island of Sumatra, Indonesia.

DUWAMISH The Duwamish are a very small Native North American group of several hundred people. They live today in northwest Washington. They speak a **dialect** of the Salishan language, which is used today by only a few old people. Many Duwamish work for lumber companies. They also fish during the summer months.

DYAWARA An **ethnic** group that lives in Mali.

DYE A subgroup of the SOMBA in Cameroon.

DYERMA see DJERMA.

DYULA (also called Jula) The Dyula are a group among the MANDINKA people that is spread over a large part of the West African grasslands. They are Muslims. There are about 1.5 million in the Ivory Coast, over one million in Burkina Faso, and over 50,000 in Mali. They speak Dyula, which belongs to the Mande family and is used by traders in most of West Africa. The word Dyula itself means "wandering trader," and that is also the traditional way the Dyula earn their living. The term "Dyula" is often used to describe all Muslim traders no matter their culture or **ethnic** background.

Before the Europeans came to Africa, the Dyula controlled trade routes from Senegal to Nigeria and from Timbuktu (in Mali) to the northern Ivory Coast. When the Europeans began to take over territory in West Africa, the Dyula spread their trading business into the new towns on the coast.

E

EAST TIMORESE The East Timorese are the people who live in the eastern part of the island of Timor in Indonesia. Experts estimate that there are now 750,000 East Timorese. East Timor was ruled for many centuries by Portugal, while West Timor was under Dutch rule. The Dutch part of Timor became Indonesian in 1949. In 1975 East Timor was taken over by Indonesia.

The East Timorese became Roman Catholics during the years of PORTUGUESE rule. They do not share the same religion with members of other **ethnic** groups in the area or with other members of their own ethnic group who live on the western part of their island. Their religion has been important to them in their efforts to define themselves as a people.

The TETUM and the ATONI are the main ethnic groups in East Timor. They speak languages belonging to the Malayo-Polynesian group of the Austronesian family.

When the Portuguese were losing power in the area, the East Timorese were strongly opposed to their territory becoming part of Indonesia. They preferred to set up their own independent state. An ongoing civil war has been fought between Indonesian soldiers and East Timorese seeking independence. Before the war there were about one million East Timorese, but many have died or lost their homes in the fighting. Many East Timorese now live in **exile** in other countries. They continue to struggle for an independent East Timor and also for rights as a minority in Indonesia.

EBRIE The Ebrie are an **ethnic** group that lives near the Ebrie Lagoon, near Abidjan, the capital of the Ivory Coast. Most are Christians.

In the mideighteenth century the Ebrie were forced to move to the area near the coast by the AGNI. In the past they never had a central government; decision-making took place in smaller villages. Today they are fully part of the Ivory Coast's modern economy and society.

ECHIRA see ESHIRA.

ECUADORIANS The Ecuadorians are the people of Ecuador, the fourth smallest country in South America. It has over 11.5 million people. Nearly 25 percent of its people are Indians, and 55 percent are *mestizo* (mixed Indian and European—mainly SPANIARDS). About one-tenth of the population came from Africa to work as slaves on plantations near the coast. Only 10 percent are Europeans (mainly Spanish), since Ecuador never attracted as many European settlers as did other South American countries. A few Ecuadorians are mulatto (mixed African and European), and others are called *montuvios* (mixed Indian and African).

The people of Ecuador are separated into groups according to their language, culture, and amount of wealth. For example, people who speak Spanish and are upper or middle class are thought of as "white" no matter what **ethnic** group they really belong to. People are called

Top: An Ecuadorian family in their Sunday clothes

Bottom: Young Ecuadorians prospecting for gold in the local river bed

Top: An Ecuadorian mother carrying her child on her back

Bottom: The tailors' section in a market in Quito, the capital of Ecuador

mestizo if they speak both Spanish and Quecha, are middle or lower class, and have a mixed culture. The Indians are people who speak either Quecha (the language of the Inca Empire that took over the area in the fifteenth century) or other Indian languages. In most cases the *mestizos* and the Indians rank far below the whites in importance and in wealth.

Peoples and regions: More than half of the people in Ecuador live in the Sierra, the Andean Mountains that are up to 9,000 feet high. The second largest number, about 46 percent, lives on the flatlands near the coast. The rest, who are mostly Indians, live in the Oriente area. This includes the eastern slopes of the Andean Mountains and the Amazon River valley. Among these Indians are the AUSHURI and the JIVARO. The Jivaro were known for fighting wars using blowpipes with poisoned darts. They then shrank the heads of the enemies they killed. Other Indian tribes have maintained a certain amount of the traditional culture of the Inca Empire. These include the PUNA, ESMERALDA, and HUANCAVILCA, who live along the coast, and the CARA, QUITU, and PURUHA, who live in the mountains. A small number (0.5 percent) of Ecuadorians live on the Galápagos Islands.

History: During the fifteenth century the Inca Indians of Peru took over most of the land that is now Ecuador. They set up one government to rule over all the tribes in the area, and taught everybody their language, Quecha. In 1525 the Incan emperor divided his kingdom between his two sons. Huascar received the south (today the areas of Peru and Bolivia), and Atahualpa received the northern kingdom of Quito. A civil war broke out between the two brothers' kingdoms. Atahualpa won, but the war made the Incas much weaker. Atahualpa converted to Catholicism in 1533 and became allied with the Spanish settlers under Francisco Pizarro. Even so, the Spanish later captured Atahualpa and put him to death. They then took control of the whole country and ruled its peoples. They founded new cities named for their heroes, such as San Francisco de Quito and Guayaquil.

Ecuadorians first started demanding their independence from Spain in Quito in 1809. After the battles that followed, the Quito territory became the republic of Ecuador in 1830.

Politics and economy: Since independence Ecuador has come under the harsh rule of many dictators. The people have had little say in how the country is run. Ecuadorians have suffered from violence caused by the army and a great deal of political turmoil. Efforts were made at the beginning of the twentieth century to modernize the country and limit the power of the Catholic religion in the government. Even so, there are still great class differences between the various peoples who live in the country. The Indians are particularly poor. Many work for others on large farms and receive very little pay. Even those Indians who own their own land have difficulty making a living because their land is worn out after many years of farming the same plots. Some Indians have moved to the poorer sections of the cities, but this only adds to the poverty problems there.

The overall economy of the country has recently been improved by modern business methods, exporting fruit, cocoa, and coffee, and mining minerals and oil. However, most of the wealth has remained in the hands of the upper classes. The life of Ecuador's poorer citizens has not really improved.

In 1979 Ecuador adopted a democratic government. Its leaders wrote a constitution that allowed all the people to vote and to have a say in how the country is run. Since then there have been regular elections in Ecuador. Even so, the Ecuadorians have remained very divided as a people because of their history of cultural, language, and class differences. A strong sense of Ecuadorian national pride has never appeared among the people of Ecuador.

EDANADAN CHETTI The Edanadan Chetti are a small **ethnic** group that lives in the southern Indian state of Kerala. They are mainly farmers.

EDDA A group among the IBO in southeastern Nigeria.

EDDE see LEBANESE.

EDIYE see BUBI.

EDO A people who live in Bendel State, Nigeria. They number about one million. Their language is part of the Niger-Congo family and is widely used in Nigeria today on radio and television. It is written with the Roman alphabet (used for English). (see also NIGERIANS)

EESTLASED see ESTONIANS.

ELSAESSER see ALSATIANS.

EFIK A group among the IBIBIO in southeastern Nigeria.

EGBA The Egba are a subgroup of the YORUBA who live around Lagos, the capital of Nigeria. Since they were the first Yoruba group to come into contact with European **missionaries**, most Egba are Christians.

In the early nineteenth century there was a civil war among the Yoruba. After the war the Egba moved from the city of Ibadan and formed a kingdom in their present lands. The BRITISH took over the area in 1914, and the Egba lost their independence. In 1918 the Egba revolted against the British, but they failed and suffered many losses.

Because they live so close to the city of Lagos, many Egba have become successful in business.

Subgroups of the Egba include the CHABA, ITSHA, KETU, MANAGO, and MANIGRI. (see also YORUBA)

EGEDE An **ethnic** group that lives in Nigeria.

EGER-UTAKAI A group among the ADYGHEANS in the North Caucasus region of Russia.

EGGAN A group among the TIV in Nigeria.

EGYPTIANS The Egyptians are the people of Egypt, the largest ARAB nation. There are 65 million Egyptians. Most are crowded into the valley of the Nile River in northern Africa. The Egyptians speak their own **dialect** of Arabic. About 94 percent are Sunni Muslims. The rest are Coptic Christians. The Copts believe that Jesus had a single nature in which the human and godly parts were combined into one.

Copts: The Copts live in Upper Egypt, Asyut, and Luxor and in Cairo and Alexandria. Since they marry only one another, they look most like the ancient Egyptians (members of the HAMITIC race). After the eighteenth century some Copts adopted Catholicism. They followed the Catholic pope in Rome but still maintained some of their Coptic traditions. Copts traditionally make a living as accountants and finance inspectors in the government. They also work as tax collectors and bankers. Even so, most have remained poor. They have complained that they are not given the same advantages as the Muslim majority in the country.

Nubians and other groups: About 200,000 Nubians originally lived in the area between Aswan in southern Egypt and the Dongola region in Sudan. When Lake Nasser was flooded, they were moved to near Kom Ombo. The Nubians became Christians in the sixth century and then converted to Islam in the fourteenth century.

Smaller **ethnic** groups in Egypt include the non-Arab BEJA. They are **nomads** who live along the border with Sudan. The BERBERS live in the Siwa area of the Western Desert where water can be found. A small number of Egyptians are

Top left: Egyptians in the El-Khalili market in Cairo, the capital of Egypt

Top right: An Egyptian fisherman mending his net

Bottom: An Egyptian butcher

BEDUIN who wander with their herds of goats, sheep, and camels in the desert.

Population and regions: Egypt has an extremely high birthrate. The country's population grows by one million people every nine months. Attempts have been made to control the population, but they have not been successful.

Cairo, with 12 million people, is a true example of a huge, overcrowded **Third World** city. It is in the center of the region of the country where people can comfortably live (the remaining 97 percent of Egypt is desert). It is located just between the Delta and the Nile Valley. There is not enough housing in Cairo for all those who want to live there, and public transportation is extremely crowded. Many people live together in small apartments. In fact, one million of Cairo's people have moved into the cemeteries. It is fitting that this settlement is called "City of the Dead." There are great extremes of wealth and poverty in the city. Beautiful neighborhoods exist right next to large slums.

About half of Egyptians live in rural areas. Most of them are simple farmers who work on the farms of rich landowners. They live in small huts that they build of mud and bricks or stones. Huts are usually arranged around an open courtyard where families keep their animals. The people living in Egyptian villages have a strong bond to one another. They celebrate religious feasts, weddings and other joyous occasions together. The mosque, a Muslim house of worship, serves as the center of the village. Even when villagers move to cities they still remain connected to their villages.

Water supply and economy: The Aswan Dam, which was finished in 1971, allows Egyptians to control their water supply. It prevents the severe water shortages that used to occur and allows farmers to water their fields at all times. Since the dam was built, there has been a 30-40 percent increase in farming production. Cotton is an important product that is sold to other countries.

Egyptians in the market

Great effort has been put into increasing the amount of goods that Egypt produces and in improving the country's income. However, because the population is growing at such a high rate, the economic growth is hardly felt by the people. Egypt earns money from fees it charges boats passing through the Suez Canal and from the salaries of several million Egyptians who work in foreign countries. However, it still needs to buy food from other countries to feed its many people, including basic staples like wheat.

History: In about the year 3100 B.C. Upper and Lower Egypt were united into one kingdom. It was ruled by a series of 30 **dynasties** of ancient Egyptian kings. During all this time the Egyptians were not overrun by other peoples and were able to develop a rich culture. They spoke a Hamitic African language that was influenced strongly by Semitic languages. They wrote using picture symbols.

Over two thousand years ago, more powerful nations swept over Egypt. It was conquered by the Assyrians, PERSIANS, GREEKS, and Romans. Each people contributed aspects of its culture to the Egyptians as they settled in the rich Nile River region. Some groups blended into the local culture. Others, particularly GREEKS and JEWS, maintained their own ways in communities that they formed in Alexandria and other cities.

When the Christians moved into Egypt in the fourth century, ancient Egypt's rich culture finally faded away. Egyptian temples were closed, and people no longer used the ancient picture symbols of their traditional language. Greek became the official language of the country. Today ancient Egyptian has been kept alive only in the language of the Copts. It is used mostly for religious ceremonies but is also spoken in some hard-to-reach villages in Upper Egypt. It is written with an alphabet similar to Greek.

When the Roman Empire was divided into eastern and western parts, Egypt came under the rule of the Byzantine or eastern Christians. The Byzantines taxed the poorest people heavily, while its leaders grew rich on the money. They also treated the Coptic Christians harshly because of their religious beliefs. The Egyptian people grew to hate the Byzantines, so they welcomed the Arabs who came to conquer the area in the year 641.

The Arabs launched an extremely strong program of spreading their culture and religion throughout Egypt. This caused a complete break with the way of life and economy that Egypt had known. Egypt now became linked with the Muslim world. More and more Arabs moved into the country, bringing their customs. Arabic became the official language in the eighth century. By about the year 1000 the Coptic language had vanished in Egypt.

Although the people had expected some relief from high taxes under the Arabs, they continued

An Egyptian artisan making pots out of alabaster stone

to be taxed severely during the Umayyad and Abbasid dynasties. The Copts tried several times to revolt, but these rebellions were put down harshly by Arab soldiers. By the eighth century Islam had become the main religion. Some of the converts had been encouraged to take on Islam by the fact that tax rates were lower for Muslims.

Egypt enjoyed a brief period of independence during the Tulunid Dynasty (868–905). Under the Shi'ite Muslim Fatimid Dynasty (969–1171) Cairo became the capital of the country, and Egypt really prospered. In the twelfth century Salah ad-Din (also called Saladin, 1137–1193) took over and formed the Ayyubid Dynasty. Salah ad-Din was a Kurd who had defeated Christian invaders in Syria and Palestine (see KURDS). He brought the traditional Sunni branch of Islam to Egypt. In 1250 the Mamelukes, who were originally Turkish slaves who had been forced to become soldiers in Egypt, took over the country.

Egyptians sitting in a coffee shop

During the time of the Christian invasions from Europe Egypt made money from good trade routes through the Red Sea. However, a better sea route around the Cape of Good Hope in South Africa was discovered in 1498. This ruined trade through Egypt. In 1516 the Ottoman Empire conquered Egypt, and three centuries of neglect of the country began. Small canals that had brought water from the Nile River to nearby fields were ignored and became useless. The country fell into terrible poverty.

Napoleon Bonaparte, the French general, invaded Egypt in 1798. Soon after Muhammad Ali, a Macedonian general, took over. He took Egypt out of the Ottoman Empire and began serious work to improve the country. He made the government, army, schools, and economy more modern. He built canals to control the waters of the Nile. This greatly improved farming and allowed Egyptians to grow cotton and

produce cotton products. He also started the very important Suez Canal. However, building the canal was much more expensive than Ali had expected. When it opened in 1869, Egypt was in economic ruin. Britain rescued the cotton industry in 1882 in order to be sure that cheap Egyptian cotton would continue to reach British cloth factories. At the same time, the British occupied the country and began to control it. Attempts by soldiers and educated people in Egypt to drive out the British only led them to take more power.

Egyptian **nationalism** continued to grow, and the people demanded that British administrators and soldiers leave their country. They called for elections for an Egyptian parliament and for Egypt to become independent. Officially, Britain gave up its formal rule over Egypt after World War I; in reality, however, they still kept a great deal of control. This led to further

Egyptians in the market

growth in Arab as well as Egyptian nationalism in the 1930s.

After Egypt attacked the new state of Israel in 1948, the Egyptian army was defeated by Israeli soldiers. This weakened the government because it led the people to feel much less respect for their king. In 1952 a group of army officers took power, drove the king away, and declared a republic in Egypt. The new leader, Gamal Abdel Nasser, set up a government that gave power only to his political party. He took many businesses and industries away from private citizens and made them the property of the government. This forced important minority communities, such as the Greeks and the Jews, to leave Egypt. With the British out of the country, Nasser took over the Suez Canal in 1956 and made it Egyptian property. This led France, Britain, and Israel to join in attacking Egypt. In the June 1967 war Egypt lost the Sinai Peninsula to Israel. Egypt continued to attack Israeli positions along the canal during the years that followed. Israel's response caused most Egyptians to move away from cities near the canal.

Egypt's next leader, Anwar al-Sadat, was concerned with improving the economic life of the country. He began the Arab war against Israel in 1973; however, he was also the first Arab ruler to sign a peace treaty with Israel. The Suez Canal, which had been closed since 1967, was reopened in 1975—a move designed to greatly improve Egypt's economy. Sadat's peace agreement with Israel led other Arab governments and groups to hate him. In 1981 he was assassinated by Muslim extremists who were opposed to peace with Israel. By the late 1980s Egyptian President Hosni Mubarak had repaired ties with other Arab countries. In the 1990–91 Persian Gulf crisis Iraq lost its key position in the Arab world. This allowed Egypt to again become the leading Arab nation.

Egyptians in traditional clothes

Culture: There are many educated Egyptians. They provide the Arab world with both religious and nonreligious books, periodicals, movies, and radio shows. However, there is growing intolerance among Islamic and very religious Coptic groups for open-minded intellectual writing and entertainment. Tensions between extremely religious and less religious groups have increased in Egypt to a very uncomfortable level. They now threaten the peace and quality of Egyptian society.

EHOTILE A group that lives in the Ivory Coast. They speak the Akan language.

EHOUE An **ethnic** group of about 33,000 that lives in the Mono Region of Togo.

EINALLU (also called Inanlu) A group among the KHAMSE in Iran.

EIPO The Eipo are an **ethnic** group of about 1,000 people. They live in eastern Irian Jaya, the Indonesian part of the island of New Guinea. Their native language belongs to the Trans-New Guinea family. They have very strong religious beliefs in magical figures who are often monsters. The live by growing different kinds of fruits and vegetables.

EJAGHAM A group among the IBIBIO in southeastern Nigeria.

EKITI A group of about 35,000 among the YORUBA who live in southwestern Nigeria. Their language belongs to the Niger-Congo family. They are related to the EFIK people.

EKKPAHIA A group among the IBO in southeastern Nigeria.

EKO A group among the YORUBA in southwestern Nigeria.

EKOT An **ethnic** group that lives in Cameroon.

EKURI A group among the IBIBIO in southeastern Nigeria.

ELEKE BEYE see NEGIDAL.

ELGEYO (also called Keyo) The Elgeyo are a group that lives on the narrow strip of land on the western bank of the Kerio River in Kenya. There are over 245,000 Elgeyo, and they make up about one percent of the country's population. Most live in the Elgeyo-Marakwet District. This is an area that ranges from 3,500 to 8,500 feet high and is surrounded by forests. They speak Kalenjin.
  Economy: The Elgeyo grow corn, nuts, coffee, wheat, pawpaws, and bananas. They also keep cattle, goats, and sheep. They consider cattle to be especially valuable, although their land was

never good for herding. They raise their cattle in ways that are similar to the NANDI people.

When there were wars in the area, it was difficult to make a living in traditional ways. This led many young Elgeyo men to join the police force and army of the European rulers. (see also KALENJIN)

EL'KAN BEYENIN see NEGIDAL.

ELLENOI see GREEKS.

ELSAESSER see ALSATIANS.

EMBU The Embu are people who live in the Embu Region of eastern Kenya on the eastern slopes of Mount Kenya. There are about 450,000 of them.

Language, religion, and culture: The Embu speak a language, which is part of the Bantu group of the Niger-Congo family. Most Embu are Christians. They belong either to European Christian groups or to African independent churches. Many Embu still keep their traditional religion.

Embu

According to their legends, they originally came from a brother and sister who had children together and were driven out of their home. They founded a new home and called their offspring the "children of Embu." Legends and story-telling are an important part of Embu culture.

The Embu have good farming land in the mountains of their territory. It includes the rich soil that was once lava that poured out of volcanoes. They grow and sell coffee and tea, and corn, beans, cabbage, and other vegetables for food.

ENCASSAR see SAHWI.

ENDE (call themselves Ata Ende) The Ende are an **ethnic** group of about 90,000 people. They live in the central part of the island of Flores in eastern Indonesia. They speak a language that is part of the Malayo-Polynesian group of the Austronesian family.

There are two separate groups among the Ende, each with their own culture: Coastal and Mountain Ende. Almost all of the 25,000 Coastal Ende are Muslims. They were influenced by the Muslim JAVANESE who arrived on their island in the sixteenth and seventeenth centuries. There are both Javanese and PORTUGUESE traces in their culture. The Mountain Ende have maintained their traditional religion and culture since they live in places that are hard for others to reach.

The Ende grow rice and corn for food and coconuts to sell. They cut and burn any natural growth to prepare their fields (slash-and-burn agriculture). When their fields get worn out, they create new ones in other areas. They also raise some farm animals.

Near the end of the eighteenth century the DUTCH set up a small Ende kingdom for a short time to keep the Portuguese from taking control of the island of Flores.

ENDO A group among the MARAKWET in Kenya.

GLOSSARY

aboriginal People that are the original or earliest known inhabitants of a place. Usually the native people of Australia.

ancestor worship Revering, praying to, or sacrificing to dead relatives. Believers think that ancestors (family members who lived before them) play a role in the life of the living.

apartheid The policy of separating groups in a country based on their race. Apartheid was practiced for many years in South Africa between black and white people.

assimilate, assimilation Adopting the culture, language, religion, etc., of another group.

atheist A person who does not believe in God.

blue-collar Factory workers or manual laborers.

boycott Refusing to buy from, attend, or take part in a business, place, or event.

cannibal A person who eats human flesh—in some cases to show that an enemy has been fully dominated; in other cases for religious reasons.

caste A group within a rigid social system in which a person's status in society is inherited. People in different castes have different privileges and restrictions and often do different work. The caste system was most widely practiced in India.

Caucasian A member of the white race.

census An official count of a population taken by a government. Some countries count different **ethnic** groups separately, and some do not.

circumcise, circumcision In males circumcision is a simple surgical procedure in which the foreskin of the penis is removed; in females it is a more serious operation in which the clitoris is removed. Children and young people are often circumcised in a ceremony that makes them full members of their society.

clan A segment of a people or ethnic group that has a common ancestor or is related by marriage. A very large extended family.

constitutional monarchy A country ruled by a king or queen whose powers are limited by a document that defines the rules of government and the rights of individuals.

coup An uprising that aims to overthrow a country's government or leader (short for the French term *coup d'état*).

crusades A series of battles fought by Christian soldiers from the eleventh to the thirteenth centuries who were trying to seize Jerusalem and the Holy Land (now called Israel) from Muslim rule.

cult A series of particular religious beliefs and practices.

deport To force people to leave the country in which they are living.

dialect A form of a language that has a different vocabulary, grammar, or pronunciation than other forms of the same language.

discrimination Treating an ethnic group or racial or any other minority unfairly.

dynasty A series of rulers; leadership is passed from generation to generation within the same family.

ethnic Describes a human group that shares race, religion, language, culture, and other traits.

exile A group or individual that is forced to leave and live away from a home country.

fascist A follower of Fascism, a political movement that called for extreme **nationalism** and the absolute power of the government headed by a very strong leader.

feudal, feudalism A legal and economic system that began in Europe in the eighth and ninth centuries in which simple farmers (**serfs**) worked for nobles and served in their armies in exchange for basic needs and protection.

forced laborers People who are made to work for others against their will, usually for very little money.

genocide The deliberate mass murder of an entire people or ethnic group.

guerrilla A war fought by small, irregular armed forces, usually for political rights, against a larger, official army or police force.

headhunting The practice among some people of removing the heads of the enemies they kill and preserving them as trophies. A person who practices headhunting is a **headhunter**.

heresy Ideas that go against the beliefs of a mainstream religion.

immigrants People who move to a new country and settle there.

Industrial Revolution A large-scale change in the Western world in the eighteenth and nineteenth centuries in which the economies of most modern countries became based on manufacturing rather than agriculture.

Islamic fundamentalism A Muslim movement whose members believe that politics and private life should be governed by a strict interpretation of the laws of Islam.

martial law Rule by the military instead of civil law. It is usually imposed by a government in times of crisis.

missionaries Individuals sent by a Christian church to a foreign country to bring Christianity, social services, and Western education to the local people. They often set up **missions** as centers with schools, hospitals, churches, and so on.

Mongoloid A member of one of the major racial groups, with yellowish skin color, straight black hair, slanting eyes, short nose, and little facial hair. They are mainly found in eastern Asia.

mosque Muslim house of worship.

myths Stories that tell how an aspect of nature or a social custom came to be.

nationalism, nationalist A strong feeling of devotion to one's country or ethnic group and its causes, which often includes the desire for political separatism or independence.

Nazi A member of the National Socialist Workers' Party that took control of Germany in

1933. The Nazis' manifesto demonstrated extreme intolerance for groups they viewed as inferior, attempted German expansion throughout the world, and accepted the absolute power of their dictator Adolph Hitler.

nomad, nomadic A member of a group that continually moves from place to place and does not live in a permanent settlement. Many nomads wander to find food and pasture for their flocks.

persecute To continually harass or treat oppressively. Minority groups sometimes suffer from **persecution**.

pilgrimage A journey (usually long) made to a holy place as a religious act.

race Part of mankind that shares physical traits such as skin color, body build, and facial features such as Caucasian ("white"), Mongoloid ("yellow"), African ("black").

radical Having very extreme political opinions.

refugee A person who had to flee for safety to a foreign country, usually during a time of war. They are sometimes forced to live in **refugee camps**.

reservation An area of public land set aside for an ethnic group, such as Native North Americans in the United States. Called **reserve** in Canada.

seminomad, seminomadic A member of a group that moves from place to place during part of the year, usually in search of grazing lands for their flocks or herds.

serfs People who live on land owned by a landlord and are required to work for him. Such an economic system is known as **feudalism**.

shrine A building, structure, or place set aside for worshipping holy beings or objects.

terrorist A person who tries to control others by carrying out violent acts that cause extreme fear. Terrorist acts are often used by **radical** groups in political struggles.

Third World Developing nations, especially in Africa, Asia, and South America.

tribes A branch of a people or ethnic group which usually descends from the same ancestor, shares customs and traditions, or has the same leader.

untouchables A member of a low **caste** in India. It was believed that touching them could make a person from a higher caste unclean.

white-collar People who work in jobs and professions that do not involve manual labor are called white-collar workers.

INDEX

Volume numbers are in bold; page numbers with illustrations or maps are italicized.

13243

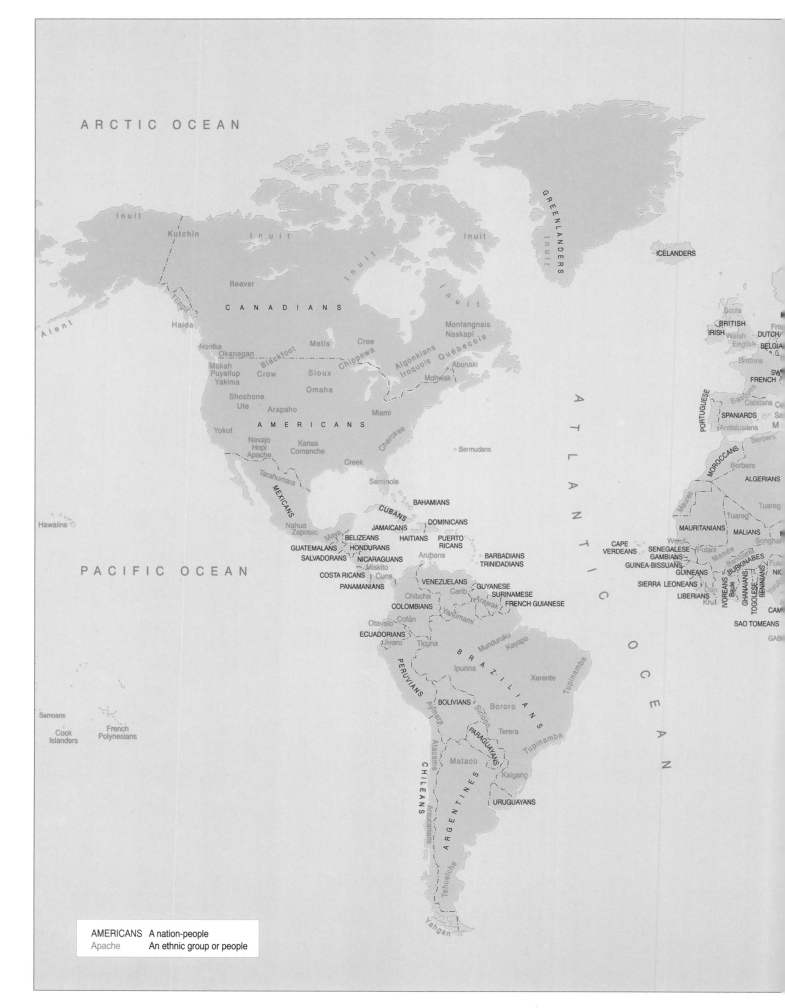

ARCTIC OCEAN

Inuit

Kutchin   Inuit

Alent

Tlingit

Haida

Beaver

CANADIANS

GREENLANDERS
Inuit

ICELANDERS

Inuit

Nootka
Okanagan
Makah
Puyallup   Blackfoot
Yakima   Crow

Metis   Cree

Sioux
Omaha

Chippewa

Inuit

Montagnais
Naskapi

Québecois

Algonkians
Iroquois   Abenaki

Mohwak

Scots
BRITISH
IRISH   Walsh
English

Bretons

Fris

DUTCH/
BELGIA

SW
FRENCH

Shoshone
Ute   Arapaho

Miami

AMERICANS
Yokut

Navajo
Hopi
Apache

Kansa
Comanche

Cherokee

Tarahumara

Creek

Seminole

MEXICANS

Hawaiins

Nahua
Zapotec

Maya
BELIZEANS
GUATEMALANS HONDURANS
SALVADORANS NICARAGUANS
Miskito
COSTA RICANS Cuna
PANAMANIANS

BAHAMIANS
CUBANS
JAMAICANS   DOMINICANS

HAITIANS   PUERTO
RICANS

Arubans

Bermudans

BARBADIANS
TRINIDADIANS

PACIFIC OCEAN

ATLANTIC

PORTUGUESE

Basques

SPANIARDS
Andalusians

Catalans Ce
Sa
M

Berbers

MOROCCANS

Berbers

ALGERIANS

Tuareg

Maures   Tuareg

CAPE
VERDEANS

MAURITANIANS   MALIANS

Welof   Fulani
SENEGALESE
GAMBIANS
GUINEA-BISSUANS   GUINEANS

Songhai

Mende

Bambari
BURKINABES
Baule BENINIANS
GHANAIANS
TOGOLESE
IVOREANS
Krul

Fula
NIC

Songhai

SIERRA LEONEANS

LIBERIANS

Dan

CAM

SAO TOMEANS

GAB

Samoans

Cook
Islanders

French
Polynesians

VENEZUELANS
Carib
Chibcha
Arawak
COLOMBIANS
Yanomami
Otavalo Cofán
ECUADORIANS
Jivaro   Ticuna

GUYANESE
SURINAMESE
FRENCH GUIANESE

Munduruku

Kayapo

B
R
A
Z
I
L
I
A
N
S

Ipurina

PERUVIANS

BOLIVIANS

Aymara

Sirjono

Bororo

Xerente

Tupinamba

Terera

Tupinamba

PARAGUAYANS

Atacama

Mataco

Kaigang

C
H
I
L
E
A
N
S

Araucanians

A
R
G
E
N
T
I
N
E
S

URUGUAYANS

Tehuelche

Yahgan

O
C
E
A
N

AMERICANS   A nation-people
Apache   An ethnic group or people